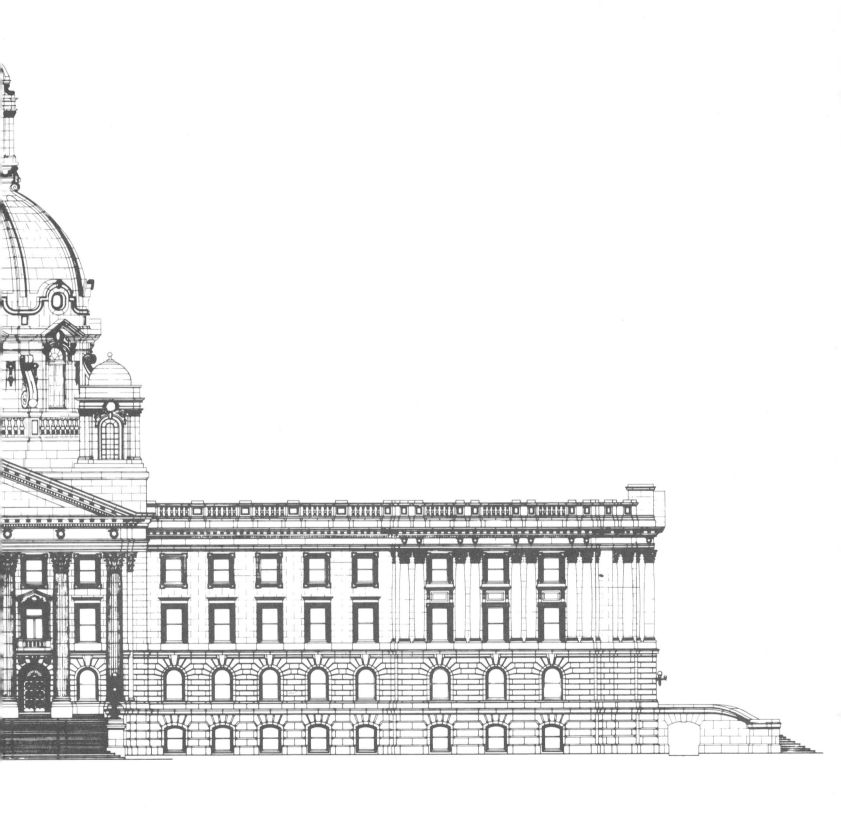

THE ALBERTA LEGISLATURE

A Celebration

Frank Dolphin

Canadian Cataloguing in Publication Data
Dolphin, Frank J. (Frank Joseph), 1928-
   The Alberta Legislature: a celebration

ISBN 0-920985-34-3

1. Parliament Buildings (Edmonton, Alta.) - History. 2. Alberta -
Politics and government. 3. Legislative Assembly - History.
I. Title.
FC3696.8.P3D64 1987   971.23   C87-091358-1
F1079.5.E3D64 1987   67307

Design: Gundra Kucy
Typesetting: Pièce de Résistance Ltée.
Separations and stripping: Color Graphics Alberta Ltd.
Printing: Commercial Colour Press Ltd.

Published by:
Plains Publishing Inc.
10316 - 121 Street
Edmonton, Alberta
T5N 1K8

Printed and bound in Canada

THE
ALBERTA
LEGISLATURE
A Celebration

Frank Dolphin

DEDICATION

To the people of Alberta through whose foresight, ingenuity and grit this Building was erected. May their strength, their wisdom and their trust guide all those who sit beneath her mighty dome.

ACKNOWLEDGEMENTS

The Author would like to acknowledge the assistance of the following individuals and organizations for their assistance in the preparation of this book:

Moragh Macaulay
Tom McIntosh
Alberta Legislature Library
City of Edmonton Archives
Edmonton Public Library
Glenbow Alberta Institute
Office of the Speaker of the Legislative Assembly of Alberta
Provincial Archives of Alberta

CONTENTS

MESSAGE FROM THE LIEUTENANT-GOVERNOR

"He builded better than he knew." (A quotation from a poem by Ralph Waldo Emerson). This phrase comes readily to mind each time I see this magnificent building. Not only does it reflect the durability and beauty of the Legislature Building itself but also the durability and strength of our Province. Hundreds of dedicated men and women have worked within these walls to make Alberta the fine Province it is today.

It would be very interesting if we could but listen to the debates of the Members of the Legislative Assembly—as well as the comments of the public—when the decision was finally reached to build a building suitable to house the seat of government. Quite a dramatic change from a school room, then a skating rink building to the present structure!

Our Province is so new compared to the other places in the world. Yet to us it seems that a hundred years is a long time. A recent visitor from an ancient country commented on the fact that we have accomplished so much in such a short time compared to his native land. I took it as a great compliment to our early pioneers whose foresight, energy and endurance started us down the road to where we are today.

We are now celebrating the 75th Anniversary of the Legislature Building. Let us appreciate our heritage and the dedication of those who have gone before us. But let us salute the future and continue the good work of our predecessors. Let us ensure that future residents of Alberta can look back and feel a sense of pride and appreciation with all that has been accomplished on their behalf. Perhaps they too will share the feeling that "He builded better than he knew."

W. Helen Hunley,
Lieutenant-Governor of Alberta

FOREWORD

This book deals with the history of Alberta's number one building. It should fill a gap in the historical writings on the Province of Alberta.

The Legislature Building of Alberta serves as a focal point in the lives of all Albertans. The 'Dome' is a symbol of government in action. While many Albertans have yet to enter under the Dome, this building is an important sight, and site, of the Albertan and Canadian way of life.

The building has a nickname—'The Leg' (pronounced *ledge*). It is a term of endearment for those of us who have been fortunate enough to walk her halls and to work within her walls. Life inside 'the Leg' can be challenging, exciting, exhausting, and on occasion a bit tedious, and yet, there is an atmosphere of awe which affects most of us who are privileged to be a part of this building which truly belongs to all Albertans.

Many people work or visit the inside of this building and many people see her from the sidewalk or from flying overhead. But 'the Leg' has many other visitors outside her walls—children who often splash in her reflecting pool; people sitting in the sun; bridal parties having their photos taken on her steps or on the grounds, demonstrators trying to voice their concerns or school children enjoying both a tour and a day off from school.

The site for the Legislature Building was well chosen—overlooking the historic water highway of the North Saskatchewan River and adjacent to Fort Edmonton. All of us are inheritors of the people who built this Province and it is only appropriate that we value our past as we continue in this present to build the future of this great Province.

On behalf of the Members of the Legislative Assembly, we offer this book as a salute to 'the Leg' and to the people of Alberta.

David Carter
Speaker
MLA - Calgary-Egmont

INTRODUCTION

Alberta's natal day fell upon Friday, September 1, 1905, and was celebrated gaily, especially in Edmonton which had been named the provisional capital until such time as it was confirmed or changed by the new legislature. Governor General Earl Grey and Prime Minister Sir Wilfrid Laurier were on hand to receive and welcome formally the newest member to the family of Canadian provinces.

There was still no elected assembly and no permanent meeting place or capital building. But plans were drawn quickly and four years later, on October 1, 1909, the same Governor General was present to lay the cornerstone and thereby launch the construction of Canada's newest and, perchance, most attractive seat of provincial government. Then, seven years after the Province's birth—almost to the day—another Governor General, the Duke of Connaught, arrived from Ottawa and officially opened the magnificent building.

Critics of the day said the cost made the new capital building an extravagance. It wasn't long, however, until most citizens were ready to declare it a sound investment. It was more than that; as an edifice symbolizing solidarity, grandeur, dignity and architectural excellence, it promised to become a focal point for pride in the new Province. With passing years and with the renovations to the landscape, public appreciation and enthusiasm for its charm continued to soar.

But about Alberta's Legislature as seen over seventy-five years, there is something more, something made distinctive by history. It is in the fact that the capital building was built on one of the oldest sites of European settlement in the Province. What a link with the history of the west half of Canada! Fort Edmonton, which survived to stand beside the new building until after the latter's completion, had been there for a century and was probably the most important post in the fur trade west of Fort William and York Factory.

Description demands superlatives in large numbers. Chief Factor John Rowand, virtual ruler of Fort Edmonton for more than thirty years, must be seen as one of the most colourful westerners of his time. He built the 'big house', the biggest thing of its kind between Fort William and the Pacific Ocean; he was responsible for the biggest ice house in Rupert's Land, capable of holding hundreds of buffalo carcasses; he laid out the first race track for horses in the West; he supervised the biggest boat building operation in the fur country and was, himself, in the words of Governor George Simpson, ''the greatest trader of them all''. If historic ground is holy ground, Alberta's Legislature has, indeed, a sure foundation.

Now, after seventy-five years, the old building appears as ageless as ever, a monument to the imagination and courage of those who authorized it, financed it, planned it and built it. It is, moreover, a monument to self-government for which the people of the area that became Alberta, fought long and hard.

What a story its old walls could tell if they could talk! They would tell of snatches of truly great oratory in the Legislative Chamber, acts of genuine statesmanship and progressive legislation in keeping with changing social, environmental, and economic conditions. They'd tell about the changes that came with oil and about an agricultural 'revolution' bringing a seventy-five-year change from ox and horse power to the adoption of four-wheel-drive mechanical monsters.

It wasn't all positive and progressive. The same old walls could tell of major disappointments, years of depression, years of drought, war years, pessimism, all of which cast shadows in the Chamber before turning to triumph and recovery. Much of the life of a province or a nation revolves around its seat of government.

It is most gratifying that the stirring record of the first seventy-five years under the dome is being captured in book form. Let there be no mistake: they were crucial years and the record, like all history, will prove useful to those who plan for tomorrow, challenging to scholars, and not without inspirational and entertainment value for everybody.

Grant MacEwan
Calgary, Alberta
March, 1987

ALBERTANS TAKE CHARGE

TIME FOR CELEBRATION

The sound of a volley from the four-gun battery of the North West Mounted Police boomed across the North Saskatchewan River valley. It echoed off the walls of Fort Edmonton, at one time the hub of the Hudson's Bay Company's fur trade. The decaying timbers of the old fort would stand for ten more years, before making way for a bowling green. Soon, a new stone building would rise near the fort to house the Alberta government.

The gunfire punctuated the final words of the oath of office read by George Hedley Vicars Bulyea. When the new Lieutenant-Governor bent to kiss the Bible, twelve thousand people cheered on the flat below McDougall Hill to welcome Alberta to Confederation.

Her birth date - September 1, 1905.

The day began with the inaugural parade down Jasper Avenue drenched in September sunshine. Governor General Earl Grey and Prime Minister Sir Wilfrid Laurier were among the special guests from Ottawa and London. Five hundred Albertans arrived on the regular Canadian Pacific train from Calgary and several hundred more travelled on a special train to celebrate the historic occasion.

The crowd lining the parade route clapped enthusiastically for the City Band, one from Strathcona and another from St. Albert. People cheered the South African veterans and the floats crammed with noisy school children. They carried signs proclaiming "The Coming Citizens, The Hope of Canada."

The pioneer city was all spruced up for the great occasion. As a reporter from the Edmonton *Bulletin* described the street scene, "Never has the city gone in so lavishly for decorations. Magnificent arches spanned the streets trimmed with evergreens, sheaves of wheat and bunting. From every business house along Jasper Avenue and from the public buildings, flags floated in the breeze and festoons of bunting swung from the windows of large blocks."

Jasper Avenue, decorated for the inaugural parade.

The lights of the Revillion Brothers' Store add a festive touch to the evening.

That night, Edmonton's downtown streets sparkled with rows of red, white and blue lights strung from the buildings. New arc lights lit the arches in the streets. Edmonton, a small pioneer community, was suddenly thrust into the role of a political capital.

STEPPING OUT

Two major social events boosted the excitement even more. The night before the inaugural, Albertans and their visitors packed the Thistle Curling Rink in downtown Edmonton for the Pre-inaugural Concert. The *Bulletin* called it "the best ever given in Edmonton."

The following evening a thousand people again packed the rink for the Inaugural Ball, the most glittering celebration in the history of the young community of eighty-five hundred people.

They liked the feel of living in the provincial capital, even if the choice of Edmonton by the federal government had still to be ratified by the Alberta legislature.

The Edmonton *Journal* reported: "In the magnificent rink auditorium, ablaze with light, a riot of colour, there gathered an assemblage that would grace any similar affair ever held in the federal capital."

The Journal noted that even with such a large attendance,"...the dancing space was not crowded. An orchestra under the direction of Walter Clark furnished music that could not be excelled and the floor was perfect." Governor General Grey stayed until after supper, presumably a late meal. "The home-going waltz was danced at two and the inaugural was at an end."

THE NEW ALBERTANS

Alberta had a population of one hundred and eighty-four thousand, eighty thousand of whom were Indians and Metis. Provincial revenues in 1905 amounted to $2,081,827, about half of that amount coming through payments from the federal government. At this point, Alberta's real wealth lay, not in cash on hand, but in the diversity and determination of its people.

The settlers were a mixed group, mainly of British and Central European immigrants, and transplanted easterners. For the most part they had left their disputes, although not all their prejudices, in their home countries. There was no class structure in Alberta. Most newcomers shared the same objectives - land and freedom.

They were ranchers, businessmen, tradesmen and ordinary people with a variety of skills. There were people on the run from the law, even a few British remittance men, problem sons told to leave Britain in return for an annual allowance. But for the most part, Albertans were hard working people looking for opportunity. Ernest Watkins caught the atmosphere of the 1900s: "Everything fell into place. This was not a totally virgin land. It had a tradition of law and order, set by the factors of the Hudson's Bay Company and immensely strengthened by the presence of the NWMP

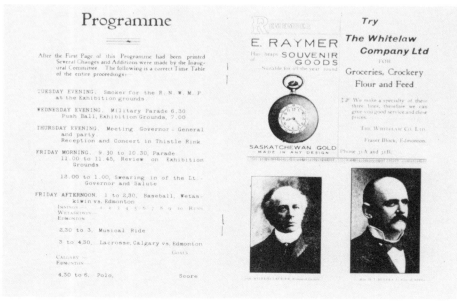

The program of events for the inaugural celebration.

... Albertans had a political freedom of choice probably unequalled before or since.''

In contrast, the future for the Indians and Metis was dismal. The Blackfoot, Blood, Cree, Peigan, Stoney, Sarcee and Chipewyan had lost their freedom to roam the prairies; the buffalo, the source of much of their food, clothing and shelter, were all but extinct. Smallpox and tuberculosis had ravaged their communities. The 1885 Northwest Rebellion, a last desperate attempt to resolve Metis land problems, ended in failure.

Native people waited until the 1970s to gain some formal recognition for their contribution to Alberta's development. Lieutenant-Governor Ralph Steinhauer, a Cree, and Sergeant-at-Arms Oscar Lacombe, a Metis, were the first native people appointed to these positions.

WAVES OF SETTLERS

In 1881, there were only a thousand settlers in the area that was to become Alberta. A combination of economic, social and political forces quickly transformed the prairie landscape from a string of Hudson's Bay Company forts and stampeding buffalo to small towns and fenced fields.

The Dominion Land Act of 1872 touched off the rush for land in the Northwest Territories. Ten years later, a hundred thousand people went homesteading. Sod shacks dotted the prairie around new communities strung along the railway line. But most new settlers ended their long trek in Manitoba and Saskatchewan, rather than continue farther west.

A world-wide economic depression put a damper on new settlement later in the 1880s. The depression ended in the '90s setting off a new round of enthusiasm for development in the west. Canadian Pacific Railway trains were rolling into Calgary, a frontier town in the heart of ranching country. Settlers now travelled west in days rather than weeks. Gone were the bone-rattling rides in oxcarts. The arrival of the railway made large-scale farming and ranching possible. Farmers and ranchers shipped their grain and cattle east; eastern businessmen shipped machinery, furniture, and everything else the settlers needed, on the trains rolling west.

By 1890, CPR crews were laying track and pounding spikes on a line to connect Edmonton with the mainline through Calgary. The branch line stopped in Strathcona, a community on the south side of the North Saskatchewan River across from Edmonton. It was named for CPR builder Donald Smith, better known as Lord Strathcona.

A sign of important economic developments to come: the first natural gas discovery had already been made in 1883 by a CPR crew drilling a water well near Medicine Hat and an oil well had been drilled up the line at Alderson. The first commercial natural gas well was in production and serving residents of the Medicine Hat area by 1890.

FEUD BEGINS

Calgary was right in the heart of the economic action, so it had what it needed to become Alberta's major city and a shot at the big prize - the provincial capital. But Edmonton wanted the capital city prize, too, and it wasn't going to give up without a battle. The Yukon Gold Rush of 1897 gave Edmonton the economic push it needed to become a commercial centre.

Fort Edmonton had been the North's supplier during the fur trade because it was the terminus of the shortest overland route to the Yukon and the whole northwest. Now Edmonton had an added advantage, sitting at the end of the railway. This made it a natural staging area and supplier for prospectors in a hurry to make their fortunes. Local businessmen saw the opportunity. They advertised Edmonton as the ''All Canadian Route to the Klondike.''

ALBERTANS TAKE CHARGE

A party prepares to leave Fort Edmonton on a Klondike expedition. John Rowand's 'Big House' is in the background.

3

Charles Smith of Houston, Texas, showed the determination of people infected with gold-fever. He invented a horse-drawn cart with whiskey barrels to replace the wheels. He claimed it would ride the lakes and rivers and endless muskeg of the north. His dream machine fell apart a couple of miles north of Edmonton.

RUNNING OUR OWN SHOW

The Hudson's Bay Company was the only government the west had known until 1870. When it turned over its lands to the federal government, parliament appointed a five-member council to govern the Northwest. Twenty-five years later, the council had evolved into an elected body of twenty-six members with its headquarters in Regina. Alberta had five seats in the Northwest Territories Legislative Assembly.

However, the Assembly was still the child of the federal government. It had limited taxation powers, no control over natural resources and crown lands, and no power to borrow money for capital construction. Major decisions, like the awarding of railway charters, were made in Ottawa. The demand for responsible government in the west became more insistent.

Haultain believed the answer was a more powerful territorial government. If, however, the federal government did grant provincial status to the west, he would accept the change but he was convinced the Territories should remain as one province. He eventually joined the pro-province forces and vigorously lobbied Sir Wilfrid Laurier to introduce the necessary legislation in the Commons.

To fit his own political situation, Laurier urged Haultain to put the demand for provincial status on hold until a redistribution of the federal parliament would give the Territories ten seats in the Commons. Haultain refused to consider the request. "The importance of provincial powers is in our opinion of much greater importance to the people of the Territories than additional representation in a parliament where failure to fulfill the duties and obligations it has been assumed with regard to the Northwest is one of our strongest reasons for demanding home rule."

Laurier turned provincial status into a federal election issue in 1904. "Elect me and I'll grant it." For westerners, there were four major issues in the campaign: the number of provinces, ownership of public lands and natural resources, the financial terms

The Legislative Assembly of the Northwest Territories (1884).

PROVINCIAL STATUS

Not everyone agreed with the move toward provincial status. Some western Members of Parliament and Senators called the idea "premature." They were joined in their opposition by Premier Frederick Haultain of the Northwest Territories, a lawyer from Fort Macleod. He was the most powerful prairie political leader at this critical time in the 1890s.

involved in joining Confederation, and the form denominational separate schools would take in a new province. The Prime Minister favoured the school system operating in Quebec. Under the same system in the west, French Catholic schools would have full and equal rights with English Protestant schools.

The school question caused a political crisis for Laurier. Clifford Sifton, the Minister of the Interior, resigned from the federal cabinet when he learned the details of Laurier's school proposal. The prime minister appointed Frank Oliver, the Edmonton newspaperman and federal Member of Parliament, to replace Sifton. Laurier watered down his proposal for separate schools to defuse the bitter campaign that could lose him seats. It worked and Laurier's Liberals won the federal election. Just as he had promised, the legislation to create two new western provinces out of part of the Northwest Territories was introduced in the Commons and received final approval on July 20, 1905.

NAMED FOR A PRINCESS

Unlike Saskatchewan, Alberta was not named in honour of the native people who had lived in the area for centuries by using one of their names for the new province. Instead, they chose to name the province for Princess Louise Caroline Alberta, the fourth daughter of Queen Victoria. The choice was made for convenience and postal efficiency. One of the four districts of the Territories already carried her name. The new province included the District of Alberta, half of the District of Athabasca and part of the districts of Saskatchewan and Assiniboia.

"I am intensely proud of this most beautiful and wonderful province being called after me," the Princess proudly announced.

Not everyone shared her enthusiasm. As far back as 1882, the Edmonton *Bulletin*, the province's first newspaper, reacted cooly to the name Alberta. "The names of... Assiniboia, Saskatchewan and Athabasca sound well and are very appropriate, but the same can hardly be said for the remaining district... There can scarcely be two opinions as to its being inappropriate as the name of a great province in a great country." But Alberta it was, and that was that.

The province was named for Princess Louise Caroline Alberta, the fourth daughter of Queen Victoria.

POLITICAL BATTLE BEGINS

Once the struggle for provincial status had been won, Laurier ignored Haultain, a Conservative, when he made the key political appointments in Alberta and Saskatchewan. Both Lieutenant-Governor George Bulyea and Premier Alexander Rutherford were Liberals. The choice of Rutherford gave Edmonton an advantage in the maneuvering for the capital.

Albertans went to the polls in their first provincial election on November 9, 1905. The Conservative Party, led by Richard Bedford Bennett, a future Canadian Prime Minister, campaigned against the policies of the Liberal government in Ottawa. The terms of Confederation had left the new provinces without control of what would become a key element in their economies. The federal government had refused to give Alberta and Saskatchewan ownership of their crown lands and mineral rights. The two provinces would wait for a quarter of a century to get what the other provinces had already received. Rutherford's Liberals stressed the need for competence in government to launch the province's development.

This cartoon appeared in the Calgary *Eye Opener* (1905).

The most immediate issue was the site of the provincial capital. Was it to be Edmonton as designated in the Alberta Act passed by the federal parliament, or should the voters demand that the new government move it to Calgary, Red Deer, Banff or some other community?

The Liberals won an overwhelming victory, twenty-two of the twenty-five seats in the Legislative Assembly. Bennett was narrowly defeated in Calgary but he would win a seat in the next election. The lopsided win set a pattern of huge government majorities that would become common in Alberta politics throughout most of its history.

Alberta had an elected provincial government. The focus now shifted to the first session of the first legislature.

ALBERTANS TAKE CHARGE

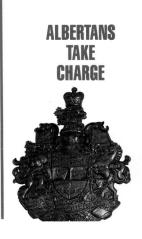

5

SIR FREDERICK W.G. HAULTAIN

Frederick Haultain arrived in Fort Macleod in 1884 from Ontario. He established a law practice and within three years won a seat on the Northwest Territories Council. Soon after, the federal government changed the name of the council to the Legislative Assembly of the Northwest Territories, reflecting the growing demand for self-government by westerners.

By 1891, Haultain was one of nine Alberta representatives and the leader of the Assembly, holding a position equal to that of a provincial premier. He originally opposed provincial status for the prairies, preferring a more powerful Territorial government. Later, he led the fight for provincial status but opposed any division of the west into several provinces, preferring instead to have one province comprising Alberta, Saskatchewan and part of Manitoba.

He didn't want provincial political parties similar to the Liberal and Conservative Parties in the House of Commons. Haultain was also opposed to the establishment of separate schools by Roman Catholics and other denominations, a right they had under the laws of the Territories. He believed religion should be taught in the church and home. However, when the new provinces of Alberta and Saskatchewan were formed in 1905, the federal government provided for separate denominational schools.

Because Haultain was a Conservative, he was passed over by Prime Minister Sir Wilfrid Laurier and his Liberal government when the appointments of a Lieutenant-Governor and Premier were made in 1905 in both Alberta and Saskatchewan. He won a seat in the Saskatchewan Legislature in 1905 but his political rights group failed to gain a majority. Haultain became the Leader of the Opposition. He was appointed Chief Justice of Saskatchewan in 1912 and given a knighthood by King George V in 1916. Haultain lived his last years in Montreal and died at the age of eighty-four in 1942. His ashes were spread on the campus of the University of Saskatchewan.

Left to right: Lieutenant-Governor of Alberta, George H. V. Bulyea; Lord Strathcona; the Honourable Alexander C. Rutherford, Premier of Alberta (September 7, 1909).

ALEXANDER CAMERON RUTHERFORD

Alberta's first premier was born near Osgoode, Carleton County, Ontario in 1857. He was a lawyer in Strathcona, across the North Saskatchewan River from Edmonton. He held two other cabinet posts, Treasurer and Minister of Education, in the new province's first government. Later, he held the portfolio of Minister of Railways.

Rutherford led the Liberal Party in Alberta to two election victories with large majorities. He was forced to resign in 1910 over a scandal involving the Alberta and Great Waterways Railway. An inquiry found the premier innocent of any personal profit in the scandal. He continued to sit in the legislature but was defeated in the 1913 election.

Rutherford served as Chancellor of the University of Alberta and one of its main libraries carries his name. He died in Edmonton in 1941.

SIR WILFRID LAURIER

Sir Wilfrid Laufier was born at St. Lin, Quebec in 1841 and became a lawyer, journalist and politician. He was Prime Minister of Canada from 1896 to 1911, and Leader of the Liberal Party for thirty-two years. One of his main attributes was the use of compromise on major issues to preserve national unity.

Laurier opposed Confederation but later accepted and supported it. During his second term as prime minister he made possible the construction of two more transcontinental railways: the Grand Trunk Pacific [his government built the eastern leg], and the Canadian Northern. Both railways went bankrupt and were amalgamated into the Canadian National Railways, a corporation owned by the federal government.

During the negotiations for the creation of Alberta and Saskatchewan, Laurier gave in to opponents of French language rights and Roman Catholic schools, just as he had done in the Manitoba School question in 1896. Separate schools in a modified form became part of the educational systems in both provinces.

Laurier led the Liberals to another term in 1908 but his influence with French-speaking Canadians suffered as a result of his compromises on education. Laurier lost the 1911 election mainly over his support for free trade with the United States. He died in Ottawa in 1919.

Sir Wilfred Laurier speaking at the Inauguration. McKay Avenue School is in the background (September 3, 1905).

FRANK OLIVER

Frank Oliver was a newspaper publisher and politician. He was born in Peel County, Ontario, in 1853. Oliver brought the first printing press to Edmonton and founded the Edmonton *Bulletin* in 1880. He was an outspoken advocate for Edmonton and helped to convince the government of Sir Wilfrid Laurier that it should be the capital of the new province.

Oliver was an Edmonton member of the Northwest Territories Council from 1883-85. He won election to the Legislative Assembly of the Northwest Territories in 1888 and 1894. He was a member of the House of Commons from 1896 to 1917. When Clifford Sifton resigned from Sir Wilfrid Laurier's government over the separate school issue, Oliver replaced him as Minister of the Interior. He was also Superintendent General of Indian affairs.

Oliver continued to publish the Edmonton *Bulletin* until 1923. He died in Ottawa in 1933.

Frank Oliver (back row, centre) with the Edmonton Hockey Club (1898).

VISCOUNT RICHARD BEDFORD BENNETT

Born in England in 1870, Viscount Bennett became a lawyer, businessman, politician and finally Prime Minister of Canada from 1930 to 1935. He won the leadership of the Conservative Party at its first convention and remained in control for eleven years.

He moved to Calgary in 1893 to become the law partner of Senator James A. Lougheed. During his early political career he won seats in the Legislative Assembly of the Northwest Territories, the Alberta Legislature and the House of Commons. Bennett was instrumental in forcing Premier Alexander Rutherford to resign over the Alberta and Great Waterways Railway scandal. Two years later he won the federal seat of Calgary East for the Conservatives.

The Dirty Thirties made his five years as Prime Minister among the most difficult for any Canadian leader since Confederation. He may be remembered best for 'Bennett Buggies,' cars pulled by horses when their owners didn't have enough money to buy gasoline. Facing the 1935 election Bennett called for unemployment insurance, progressive taxation and other measures to ease the effect of the Depression. The New Deal measures didn't gain voter support for him in the way they had done for President Roosevelt in the United States.

Bennett returned to England and died in 1947.

A HOME FOR THE LEGISLATORS

FIRST SESSION BEGINS

A sharp wind tugged at coat collars as Edmontonians and thousands of visitors hurried along 102 Street to the Thistle Curling Rink, north of Jasper Avenue on March 15, 1906. Every hotel and boarding house in Edmonton and Strathcona was booked with people from the Peace River Country to the American border. They rushed to get one of the four thousand places at the opening of the First Session of the Alberta Legislature.

The clip-clop of horses' hooves brought the honour-guard to attention. Lieutenant-Governor George Bulyea's carriage rolled to a stop and he stepped down quickly to perform the brief ceremonies in front of the rink before going inside to read the province's first Speech from the Throne.

Workers had spent two days converting the plain-looking rink into an attractive place for yet another historic happening. Flags and banners hung from the ceiling. Sawdust covered the curling ice and the guests sat on pews from nearby churches. The twenty-three Liberal members and two Conservatives listened intently to the speech outlining the steps Premier Alexander Rutherford planned to organize his newly elected government.

He would carry much of the load himself. In addition to his job as Premier, Rutherford was also the Provincial Treasurer and Minister of Education. C.W. Cross of Edmonton became the Attorney General; W.H. Cushing of Calgary, Minister of Public Works; W.T. Finlay of Medicine Hat, Minister of Agriculture

The opening of Alberta's first legislature at the Thistle Curling Rink (March 15, 1906).

and Provincial Secretary; and L.G. DeVeber of Lethbridge, Minister Without Portfolio. Charles Fisher, the member for Cochrane, was elected the Assembly's first Speaker.

The most important piece of business - the one that was on everyone's mind - didn't get a mention in the throne speech. Rutherford had every intention of quickly settling the location of the capital. The Alberta Act, passed by the House of Commons in Ottawa, had designated Edmonton but the Alberta Legislature could overturn that decision and choose another city or town.

DOWN TO WORK

Once the opening ceremonies were completed, the Assembly moved to the third floor of McKay Avenue School, on the brow of the hill at 105th Street, for the daily sittings. The members were relatively young, with the average around forty-five. Although a few were pioneers, none of them were born in Alberta. Most had headed west from Ontario. One of the real characters was Arlie Brick, the member for Peace River. He travelled to one session by sleigh with a small cabin on the back, pulled by two moose.

Plenty of political manoeuvering was underway in the background to consolidate Edmonton's position as the capital. Government departments temporarily established offices for their one hundred employees in the Empire Block at 101st Street and Jasper Avenue and in other buildings around the city. Within a few months the civil servants moved into the newly constructed Terrace Building at 96th Avenue and 106th Street. The Assembly held its 1908 session in the Annex next door. The Terrace Building had been designed for conversion to suites once the new Legislature Building was built. But its temporary status lasted until 1961 when the building was demolished to make way for a new office building.

William Aitken, a civil servant who worked in the Terrace Building, remembered the night in 1910 he listened at the Annex door to the famous five hour speech by R.B. Bennett over the railway scandal. He had even fonder memories of the professional baseball games at Diamond Park, just down the hill. Historian Tony Cashman interviewed Aitken, "They played the games in the afternoon but I don't think I ever missed one. I suppose my boss thought I was out checking a road."

Alberta legislators on the steps of McKay Avenue School (1906).

McKay Avenue School.

THE BATTLE FOR THE CAPITAL

Edmonton and Calgary were intense rivals for the seat of government. Their political differences heightened that competitiveness; Calgary's politics were mainly Conservative, Edmonton's Liberal, and for good reason. Many Calgarians were dependent on the railway, a creation of the federal Tories, for their livelihood. Bennett, the provincial Tory leader, was the CPR lawyer. The combination created strong Conservative support in the south. The political landscape was different in central and northern Alberta. Farmers in these areas disliked the CPR for what they thought were the company's excessively high freight rates. For that reason they supported the Liberals. Little wonder the province was split.

The fight became even more bitter when Frank Oliver, a loyal Edmontonian, a Liberal, and the federal Minister of the Interior, established the boundaries for the province's twenty-five provincial constituences. Most of them stretched east and west across the province from British Columbia to Saskatchewan. Each community was in a single constituency.

In the Edmonton area they were drawn so that the city became a hub with the constituencies radiating outward, like spokes in a wheel. Edmonton voters were represented, not by a single member, but by six. Calgarians screamed the fix was on. The Calgary *Herald* likened the constituencies to "the tentacles of an octopus."

This window display in the McDougall & Secord Store shows the rivalry between Edmonton and Calgary over the location of the provincial capital (September 1, 1905).

12

OLD RIVALRIES NEVER DIE

Hansard, Aug. 29, 1986

MR. PAYNE: Mr. Speaker, ... In view of the anticipated victory by the resurgent Calgary Stampeders next Monday, could the Deputy Premier advise the Assembly as to the economic implications of the government's previous loan guarantees in light of the Stampeders' remarkable turnaround on both the balance sheet and the football field.

MR. RUSSELL: Seriously, Mr. Speaker, that is a very happy situation coming at a good time in life of the community of Calgary, a nice kind of community effort success story that we like to hear about. It is correct that when the community-owned team was in danger of failing last year, the government - on the initiative of our Premier, who has some interest in the game - stepped in with a loan guarantee of $1,000,000. ... There is one more step to follow in the plan of action which may not particularly please the Premier. Monday, the Eskimos are going to be annihilated.

MR. SPEAKER: A reasoned supplementary.

MR. PAYNE: ... could the Premier indicate his policy position today as to the outcome of Monday's game in Calgary?

MR. SPEAKER: With all due respect to former quarterbacks of the Eskimos, the Chair recognizes the Member for Athabasca-Lac La Biche followed by the Member for Calgary Buffalo.

MR. GETTY: On a point of order, Mr. Speaker.

MR. SPEAKER: Points of order will be recognized at the end of question period.

Later

MR. GETTY: I've been thinking about that point of order, Mr Speaker. The hon. Deputy Premier having raised the fact of the annihilation of the Edmonton Eskimos by the Calgary Stampeders, I only want to advise the House that I'm reconsidering the position of Deputy Premier.

Edmonton and Calgary newspapers took up the fight. During the 1905 provincial election campaign, the Edmonton *Bulletin* pointed out that Rutherford and Bennett were pledged to make their own cities the capital. "Therefore, every vote cast for an opposition candidate, is a vote against maintaining the capital in Edmonton."

As far back as January, 1905, before the province received federal approval, the Calgary *Herald* had confidently predicted Calgary would be named the capital. "Yesterday the western representatives were in caucus and there seems to be little difference of opinion among them as to the economy of the proposition."

These weren't the only proposals for the legislature's consideration. One came from Speaker Fisher of Banff. Among his arguments was the novel contention that in the case of an attack against Alberta by some unidentified enemy, Banff could be turned into an impregnable fortress.

The politicians couldn't ignore a bid from Red Deer. If there had to be a compromise, the community half way between the two cities seemed like the ideal political solution. The Premier and members decided to see for themselves what Red Deer offered. As they stepped from a railway saloon car, local residents greeted them with three hearty cheers. Red Deer as the capital of Alberta didn't seem nearly so far-fetched after the friendly reception, a tour of possible sites for new government buildings, and a sumptuous dinner.

The Red Deer *Advocate* reported, "After singing Auld Lang Syne and God Save the King the company broke up at 4:45 a.m., each and all expressing themselves at the perfect success of the banquet and the visitors were loud in their expression of pleasure and satisfaction of their visit to the town."

But nothing could break Edmonton's hold on the capital. A final attempt by southern Alberta members to move it to Calgary was defeated by a vote of sixteen to eight. Edmonton was the seat of the provincial government. This issue was settled but the rivalry between the two cities continued to smoulder, quickly bursting to the surface in the decades to follow whenever their was a prize to be won in the boardrooms, political backrooms and on Edmonton and Calgary's hockey rinks and playing fields.

A HOME FOR THE LEGISLATORS

"Edmonton House", painted by Paul Kane (1846).

CHOOSING A SITE

The next decision - the choice of the most appropriate site for the new Legislature. What better spot than near Fort Edmonton, now abandoned and crumbling? Rutherford and his cabinet favoured the high ground overlooking the fort and near the site of Hardisty House, the residence of the last Fort Edmonton factor. Edmonton health officials used the abandoned house for a hospital during a flu epidemic in 1906. Once the epidemic had run its course, they burned down the building.

The Edmonton *Bulletin* welcomed the choice "... the site could not be excelled." The newspaper viewed the plateau on the river bank where the fort sat as a link between Alberta's fur-trading past and its future as "a prosperous civilization."

Not everyone liked the government's choice. The Edmonton *Saturday News* argued the Legislature would be too close to the CPR's proposed High Level Bridge.

"A good appearance will not make up for the noise which trains passing over such a structure must create... The railway will be a nuisance and future generations will never cease to wonder what could have induced the administration of the day to select such a site."

Premier Rutherford swept aside all criticism. The province sealed the deal on October 11, 1906, by purchasing twenty-one acres from the Hudson's Bay Company for $4,000 an acre. The near reverence for Fort Edmonton was soon forgotten. Just eight years later, the Sifton government authorized the demolition of the fort's remaining palisades and bastions to make way for the construction of a bowling green. The government tried to still its critics by promising to reconstruct the fort in another location, a promise it failed to keep. Fifty years later, Fort Edmonton was reconstructed in the river valley, two miles west of the Legislature, the heart of a heritage park.

KING OF THE FRONTIER

A Touch of Class

John Rowand introduced a quality of life to Fort Edmonton unknown in the string of Hudson's Bay Company outposts throughout the west. He was appointed Edmonton's chief factor in 1826. He built a family home, known as the 'Big House' or by some as 'Rowand's Folly.' It boasted glass windows rarely seen in the west, transported in barrels of molasses from eastern Canada.

Life wasn't all furs and tough bargaining. Rowand found time to indulge his main outside interest - horse racing. He bred his own race horses and built the west's first race track, outside the fort. The factor liked to travel the fur routes and far beyond. One winter he went to California and Hawaii.

Tragic Death

Rowand's death in 1854 was as spectacular as his life. He tried to stop a fight between two of his men by stepping between them. The strain was too much and he dropped dead, apparently from a heart attack. Sir George Simpson, the Governor of the Hudson's Bay Company, fulfilled Rowand's wish that he be buried in Montreal. He packed Rowand's bones in a rum cask and labelled it 'Salt Pork', so the highly superstitious voyageurs wouldn't realize what they were transporting and throw the cask overboard. Rowand's bones travelled by ship through Hudson Bay to England and eventually made the return voyage to North America for burial in Montreal's Mount Royal Cemetery.

RUTHERFORD FORCED OUT

The members were still six years away from their first debate in the new Legislature. While the building's design and construction were a prime concern for the government, plenty of other decisions had to be made. Forty thousand immigrants were arriving each year. Edmonton was so crowded that two thousand people and probably more were living in tents in 1907. Albertans needed schools, telephones and railways.

Calgary lost another major prize to Edmonton - the University of Alberta. Rutherford didn't quite give it to Edmonton. Rather, he chose Strathcona, across the river. However, the community of 3,500 was soon swallowed up by Edmonton.

The young government plunged into two major ventures - telephones and railways. It broke the Bell Telephone monopoly in the province by establishing Alberta Government Telephones. Then it guaranteed the construction of 1,761 miles of branch lines for the Canadian Northern Railway and the Alberta and Great Waterways Railway Company. A scandal over railway bonds in 1910 wrecked Rutherford's government and forced him to resign. Arthur Sifton, the Chief Justice of the province, became Alberta's second Premier.

A HOME FOR THE LEGISLATORS

GETTING THE RIGHT DESIGN

Against this background of tough, unyielding politics, the Legislature project was moving ahead. The Public Works Department decided it would handle the design for the largest and most expensive construction job ever attempted in Alberta without a public tender. Edward C. Hopkins of Calgary was appointed provincial architect in 1906 and almost immediately submitted his proposal for a new Legislature. The design, featuring a large central dome with eight-sided towers on the wings, strongly resembled the British Columbia Legislature. In fact, what the public saw was the actual B.C. design. Hopkins submitted a second design but government officials rejected it.

In April, 1907, the Public Works Department hired an American, Allan Merrick Jeffers, as the province's chief architectural draughtsman. By September of the same year, he had the job of Provincial Architect. The decision to put the Legislature's design into the hands of an American caused an uproar. Jeffers' manner helped to fuel the controversy. He was secretive and refused to listen to local ideas. This led to rumours he was using the design of the State Capitol Building in Minnesota - rumours that Jeffers later refused to confirm or deny. However, the criticism faded when he became a naturalized British subject in 1910.

Studies of the Alberta Legislature leave no doubt that it was influenced by the design of American capitol buildings. Jeffers was born in Rhode Island and studied at the Rhode Island School of Design. The Rhode Island State Capitol, which featured the Beaux-Arts Style, certainly would have been a strong influence on him. Its most distinctive feature was the central dome, based on the dome of St. Paul's Cathedral in London. At the very least, Jeffers would have been familiar with that style and method of designing such buildings.

Another reason to believe there was strong American influence on the Alberta design was the visit in 1907 by Public Works Minister Cushing to the Minnesota and Wisconsin State Houses to gather ideas. Later the same year, Premier Rutherford visited St. Paul to pick up more ideas from the Minnesota building.

The Alberta Legislature's design is a simplified Beaux-Arts Style. Among the common elements of the style found in the building are the T-shaped plan, with the main portico supported by six large, fluted Corinthian columns. Present-day architects are puzzled by the triangles over the east and west entrances which have been left unfinished. No one knows why.

The interior of the building has coupled half columns and a combination of round and flat arched windows in the same elevation, and a grand flight of stairs. The bar of the 'T' contains offices for cabinet ministers and members. The rotunda connects the wings and leads up the grand staircase to the Legislative Assembly. The entrance to the Legislature Library is behind the main stairway.

Allan Merrick Jeffers, architect of the Alberta Legislature.

Although Jeffers signed all changes in the design, government officials consulted other engineers and architects. These included John Chalmers, the provincial structural engineer; William Fingland, an architect; and Percy Nobbs, Professor of Architecture at McGill University in Montreal, who made final changes to the preliminary sketches.

The Legislature's main architect resigned from the provincial government before the building was completed. The City of Edmonton hired Jeffers to build the Civic Block, which served as the City Hall for almost forty years. He also designed McDougall School in Calgary, now used as a provincial government centre. He finally returned to the U.S. to build movie sets in Hollywood.

The other major architect of the Alberta Legislature was Richard P. Blakey, Jeffers' assistant, who replaced him after his resignation. He made substantial changes to Jeffers' plans. Blakey created the view of the main doors of the Assembly which can be seen by visitors as they enter the front doors of the building. He also designed a dome within the dome by lowering the roof and changing the proportions of the rotunda.

Corinthian columns dominate the north facade of the Legislature.

Following page, left to right:
St. Paul's Cathedral, London, England; Rhode Island State Capitol, Providence, Rhode Island; Minnesota State Capitol, St. Paul, Minnesota; Wisconsin State Capitol, Madison, Wisconsin.

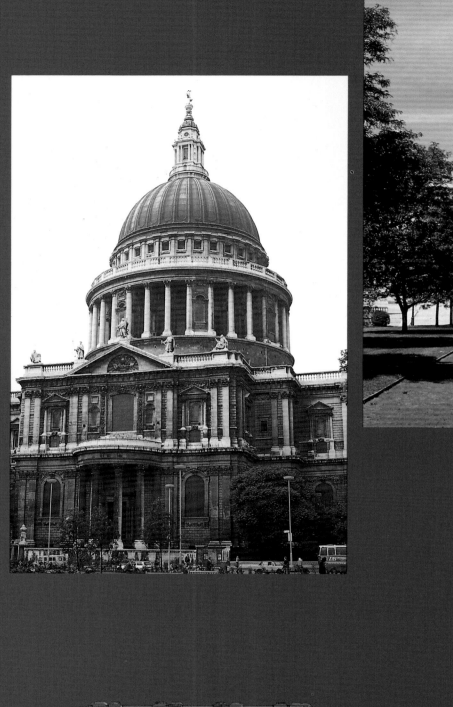

CONSTRUCTION BEGINS

The roar of a steam shovel in August, 1907, announced the start of the excavation, measuring 427 feet by 290 feet. The government tendered all the contracts and the work was done mainly by day labourers. Workers began the concrete work on the foundation in the third week of October, two months before the public had a chance to see the final design.

No one is quite sure how much quicksand the construction workers hit when they put in the footings. One construction summary, written in 1947, mentioned the problem. "Due to the nature of the soil having quicksands in it, we had to drive concrete piles before footings were set in. These footings were all embedded in large channel beams." This unsigned report doesn't suggest the quicksand ran up the cost but others blame it as one of the main factors for going well over the original estimate of $1,250,000. No one seems quite sure just how much the Legislature did cost. Some reports go as high as $4,000,000.

Steel girders went up in 1909 and stone masons slowly filled in the skeleton. They used granite from Vancouver Island for the exterior of the first storey; greyish yellow Paskapoo sandstone from the Glenbow quarry near Calgary and some larger slabs from Ohio completed the exterior of the building. The latter were imported because finding flawless slabs in the Glenbow quarry became too expensive.

Governor General Earl Grey laid the cornerstone on October 1, 1909. Under the stone were copies of the three Edmonton newspapers publishing at that time, a complete set of building plans, coins and currency, a copy of the pay sheet, and a list of the officials who supervised the construction.

The excavation site (September, 1907).

The Legislature and High Level Bridge under construction (1912).

Cranes dominate the skyline at the construction site.

20

Cutting ice on the North Saskatchewan River. The buildings of Fort Edmonton and the Legislature and High Level Bridge under construction are visible in the background.

Scaffolding covers the nearly-completed Legislature

Years later when it was time to make renovations, government officials must have wondered why one of the two full sets of plans was placed under the corner stone. The second set was destroyed in a fire at the Terrace Building in the 1920s. Workers had to re-draw the plans and used mechanical snakes to trace the wiring.

An archway decorated with carved wreaths.

A HOME
FOR THE
LEGISLATORS

GRAND OPENING

Construction was still in full swing in November, 1911, when the members moved in for their first session in the new Legislature. But just three months later, workers were back in the Assembly repairing cracks in the fresh plaster and in the library on the floor below. Already members were complaining about the poor acoustics in the Assembly, a complaint that persisted until a sound system was installed in the '60s. Even worse than the cracked plaster, an architectural error forced rebuilding of the arches supporting the ceilings of the corridors outside the assembly.

The rush was on to complete as much of the building as possible for the official opening on Sept. 3, 1912. When the Duke of Connaught, the new Governor General, arrived, the main entrance, rotunda, assembly, dining room and most of the east wing were finished.

A sign that everything wasn't quite finished was that the Legislature's oak doors, hand carved in England, had no locks.

When the Governor General was supposedly unlocking the doors, someone else was on the inside pulling them open. Fortunately there was no television to give Albertans a close-up of the arrival. That bit of play-acting didn't prevent provincial officials from presenting him with a replica of the key to the main doors. It was made of gold from the North Saskatchewan River with an inscription of the Provincial and Canadian Coats-of Arms. At last, the new Alberta Legislature was formally and fittingly opened.

Since that time, the one question probably asked more often than any other, "Why did those first Albertans build such a grandiose building in an isolated frontier community?"

Diana Bodnar gave one explanation, " ... geographically isolated communities attempted to link their prairie environment, architecturally at least, with American and European centres of cultural, economic, and political activity. They wanted to prove that they were respectable, that they were progressive, and equal."

The official opening of the Alberta Legislature (September 3, 1912).

22

The construction crew packed away its tools in 1913. Premier Arthur Sifton moved into his office on the third floor of the east wing. As civil servants moved from the old buildings around Edmonton, it quickly became apparent the grand new building wasn't large enough to house everyone. The overflow stayed in the Terrace Building. John Stocks, the first Deputy Minister of Public Works must have been keeping a low profile. When he saw the preliminary sketches back in 1907, he knocked 30 feet off each wing. "All those offices? They'll never fill them."

The Edmonton *Journal* couldn't resist a shot at the government architects and planners. "Barely had the staffs been transferred from the old buildings, commonly, but affectionately, known as 'the barracks,' than the Department of Public Works had to turn to its usual devices and tear out what it had put in, and construct that which it left out."

Too small or not, Alberta had a new Legislature Building.

The Prince and Princess of Wales visit Alberta (1983).

A HOME FOR THE LEGISLATORS

Right: An east view of the Legislature. Below: Past meets present: the Hudson's Bay Company fort and the newly completed Legislature (1913).

Above: The Legislative Assembly of Alberta (1918).
Below: The Legislative Assembly of Alberta (1983).

A HOME
FOR THE
LEGISLATORS

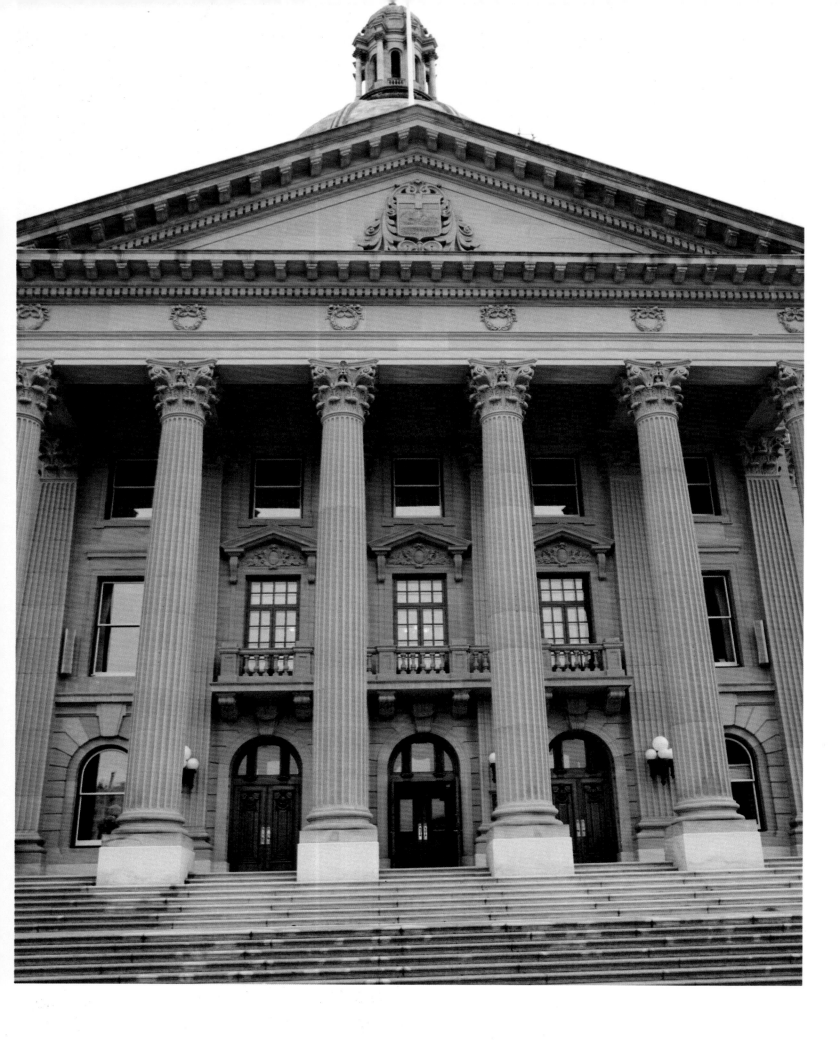

THROUGH ALBERTA'S FRONT DOOR

NOT QUITE AT HOME

Workers like James Millar and his son John were proud to be building Alberta's new Legislature. They hauled the sandstone and marble in their horse-drawn wagons from railway cars on a 700 foot siding along the face of the hill to the construction site overlooking old Fort Edmonton. Their labours gave them a feeling of involvement in something historic and lasting, but it would be a long time before they could feel at home inside the building that belonged to them and all Albertans. Years later, the two men explained to relatives in Edmonton, ''Outside was for workmen; inside for gentlemen.'' Many Albertans shared that attitude.

Ray Speaker, the longest sitting member now in the Assembly, found the same reluctance to enter the building even in the 1960s. The member for Little Bow in southern Alberta often talked to people who lived along his daily walk to the Legislature. Many had never been in the building.

''They were afraid to go inside. I tried to tell them they owned it.'' He noticed, too, the Assembly's galleries were rarely full, except when there was keen interest in an issue and the politicians were producing the best entertainment in town. In contrast with the thousands of students who now come from every constituency, few school districts in the 1960s could afford the luxury of a day at the Legislature.

The building's popularity grew when the province's economy improved. Fifteen thousand visitors a year passed through the front doors in the late 1950s. By the mid-1980s the figure reached almost sixty thousand people from across Canada and around the world. Most Canadian visitors came from outside Alberta. Americans made up a third of the foreign visitors. The multilingual guides add a welcome touch, often greeting the visitors in their own language. Strangely enough, many Edmontonians make their first visit to the Legislature only when they bring guests.

EYE ON THE DOME

The massive dome, 176 feet high, is the most striking architectural feature of the Legislature, one that captures the attention of visitors long before they arrive. The attention of maintenance officials is riveted almost constantly on the dome. They're watching for falling bits of mortar, a signal that the sandstone blocks and terracotta upper surface are shifting.

The building underwent its first major facelift in 1954 when highriggers crawled over the dome to replace chipped and missing calking. They repeated the job in 1977. To the amazement of engineers from other parts of North America, there were no cracks in the dome itself despite quicksand under the foundation.

In 1985 the workmen were back on the dome waterproofing the joints. Bill Kreibom, the building superintendent, blamed the cracking on the high humidity from the fountain below the dome and the cold dry air outside causing alternate freezing and melting. Electronic probes on the west side of the dome monitor temperature and humidity changes and record any slight movement in the stones.

GOING UP

Climb the fifty-five steps from the fifth floor and you arrive at the 'Palm Room'. The main features are eight arched windows, topped by eight bullseye windows or portholes, copied from the Brazilian pavilion at the 1904 St. Louis World's Fair. The gallery gets its name from five palm trees growing in huge tubs. They were started

Looking south from the lantern of the dome.

The dome gallery, or "Palm Room". These trees were started from seeds, a gift from the State of California.

from seeds sent as a gift of the State of California in 1922.

Another ninety-five steps take you to the "lantern," a cupola which houses a beacon to signal when a night sitting is in progress. One story claims the light was put there mainly to calm the fears of members' anxious wives when their husbands didn't appear for dinner. The cupola provides a spectacular view of the river valley and the city, but it's no longer open to visitors.

EASTER EGG COLOURS

One day in 1956, visitors and civil servants gasped as they watched a new colour scheme transform the dome and the walls below. The familiar off-white quickly disappeared. Painters perched on scaffolds painted the dome a sky blue with dashes of red, green and brown on the rounded ceiling below the dome. The walls and arches down to the third floor turned platinum grey to blend with the marble of the Corinthian columns. The walls of the corridors around the central core got a coat of cocoa brown to accentuate their arches and columns.

Left: Flowers add a welcome splash of colour to the grey marble fountain.
Above: The north view from the dome.

28

Above: The fountain and grand staircase.
Right: The dome, looking up from the rotunda.

L.G. MacDonald, the public works architect in charge of the refurbishing, cautioned the critics, ''Just wait and see.'' He contended that the white robbed the dome of character. The bright colours would bring out the fine plaster ornamentation. The finished job got mixed reviews. Opposition members tagged it the ''ginger bread house.'' The paint job survived until 1987.

Architect Brian Woolfenden of Woolfenden Hamilton Brown Architectural Group supervised a $110,000 contract ''to restore the pristine beauty of the rotunda and allow the architecture of the space to be self-expressive.'' Two colours were selected for this restoration: white, to emphasize the volume of the space; and grey-green, to enhance specific features of the design and to compliment the marble columns and walls. The painters completed the work in six weeks.

Clockwise from top left: Flags of battalions which served in the World Wars hang in the rotunda; The rotunda, looking west from the entrance; Bronze memorial plaques honour those who served in the First and Second World Wars; The massive bronze light fixtures which hang in the rotunda must be lowered in order to change the bulbs; A World War II Honour Roll in the rotunda; The light grey marble of the grand staircase is accented by the darker grey of the balustrade, which is of eighteenth century English design; The rotunda, seen from the front door by the tour desk.

HISTORY'S SOUVENIRS

The main floor of the rotunda leads visitors to the grand staircase and to the east and west wings of the building. The pillars and base of the rotunda, the halls and the main section of the staircase were finished with light grey marble from Phillipsburg, Quebec. Dark grey Italian marble was the choice for the railings of the staircase, the fountain and the third floor. Artisans came from Italy in 1911 to lay the terrazzo floors.

Standing near the main entrance are two life-size bronze statues: Princess Louise Caroline Alberta, for whom the province was named; and Crowfoot, Chief of the Blackfoot Confederacy, one of the west's greatest Indian leaders.

In 1927, the prospect of a visit by the Prince of Wales rushed the mounting of two bronze tablets, one on each side of the main stairway leading to the Assembly. One tablet lists an honour role of 235 provincial civil servants who served in World War One. The second contains the names of twenty-seven men killed in action.

The Royal Tour of King George VI and Queen Elizabeth in 1939, the first cross-Canada visit by a reigning monarch, was marked by the construction of a temporary fountain and flower bed in the centre of the rotunda. The government splurged $2,200 on a new green carpet to replace the threadbare red one which had covered the Assembly floor. After the visit, the fountain was removed and the floor well re-opened to restore the view of the dome from the lower floor.

In 1951, two more memorial plaques were hung in the rotunda to commemorate the civil servants who served in World War II. Twenty-seven government employees gave their lives in the Canadian armed forces.

Flags bearing the regimental colours and King's colour of battalions, which served in both World Wars, hang in the rotunda to honour the province's servicemen

and women. They are: the White Ensign of the Royal Canadian Navy, HMCS Nonsuch; the 218th Canadian Infantry Battalion, amalgamated to form the 8th Canadian Railway Troop; the 51st Canadian Infantry Battalion, amalgamated to form the 2nd Reserve Battalion, Edmonton Regiment; the Loyal Edmonton Regiment, 3rd Battalion Princess Patricia's Canadian Light Infantry, which became the Loyal Edmonton Regiment, 4th Battalion PPCLI; the 66th Canadian Infantry Battalion, amalgamated to form the 2nd Reserve Battalion, Edmonton Fusiliers; the 194th Canadian Infantry Battalion, Edmonton Highlanders, amalgamated to form the 9th Reserve Battalion; and the 202nd Canadian Infantry Battalion, amalgamated to form the 3rd Reserve Battalion, Edmonton Fusiliers.

FOUNTAIN RETURNS

The province marked a visit by Queen Elizabeth and Prince Philip in 1959 by restoring the fountain in the centre of the rotunda. A floral arrangement around the fountain from the government greenhouse brought an added touch of colour. The splashing water was a delight for visitors but a headache for the maintenance staff.

An elusive leak produced a wet spot on the basement ceiling below that stubbornly re-appeared after workers ripped up the the floor several times to repair it.

Woolfenden has recommended the removal of the fountain and reopening of the floor well. In his view, the fountain creates too much noise, and evaporation causes much of the problem in the dome. Unfortunately, removing the fountain would eliminate an interesting effect on the fifth floor. The sound converges in one spot giving visitors the impression they are standing under the fountain. Woolfenden favours a circular stairway to the lower floor and the installation of a much smaller fountain there. The lower area could be converted into an attractive gallery for historical artifacts and portraits, opening it for public use.

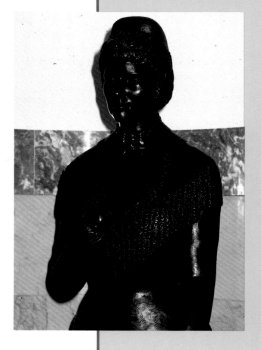

Two Special People

Two life-size bronze statues of a woman and a man stand in niches on the north wall of the rotunda. They are Princess Louise Caroline Alberta, who gave her name to the province, and Chief Crowfoot, an Indian leader of the Blackfoot Confederacy who persuaded other chiefs to sign Treaty Seven, an agreement necessary to the formation of the province.

The statue of Princess Louise is by Olle Holmsten, formerly of Calgary. It was cast by Studio West of Cochrane. The statue of Chief Crowfoot was created by Cornelius Martens of Coaldale and cast by Sculptcast of Edmonton.

A Royal Name

Twenty-seven years before Alberta became a province, a large area of the Northwest Territories bordering on the Rocky Mountains was named after Princess Louise Caroline Alberta. When Prime Minister Sir Wilfrid Laurier combined the area with part of Athabasca, Saskatchewan and Assiniboia, the new province became "Alberta." Lake Louise, the most spectacular lake in the Rockies, also bears the name of Queen Victoria's fourth daughter.

Princess Louise Caroline Alberta was born in 1848. She married the Marquis of Lorne and accompanied him to Canada when he was named Governor General in 1878. Illness prevented her from travelling with her husband to the largely unsettled territory named in her honour.

Princess Louise and the Marquis were interested in education and the arts. They helped to establish the Royal Canadian Academy of the Arts. He founded the Royal Society of Canada. When Princess Louise died in 1939, Prime Minister Mackenzie King sent a telegram to the royal family, "Canada has lost a true friend who never failed to retain a very special interest in the country which was so much a part of her earlier life."

A Native Leader

Crowfoot was born a Blood in 1830 but grew up among the Blackfoot. He received an ancestor's name, Crow Indian's Big Foot, later shortened by interpreters to Crowfoot, by striking a painted tipi in a Crow camp during a battle. A renowned warrior, he went into battle nineteen times and was wounded six times. His exploits included the killing of a grizzly bear with a lance while many of his people watched.

Crowfoot became chief of the Big Pipes band and one of three head chiefs of the Blackfoot. He made peace with the Cree and supported the Northwest Mounted Police when they arrived to hunt down the whiskey traders. Crowfoot was one of the signators of Treaty Number Seven and through his influence persuaded other chiefs to agree to the establishment of Indian reserves.

The traders, police and missionaries greatly respected Crowfoot for his wise leadership and diplomatic skills. His influence with federal government officials often resulted in better treatment for Indians. Crowfoot died near Blackfoot Crossing in southern Alberta in 1890.

Top: Portraits of King George V and Queen Mary hang in the portrait gallery.
Above: Two thousand tons of marble were used in the construction of the Legislature.

WHAT PEOPLE ASK

Visitors want to know many of the details of the Legislature's architecture and construction. Here are a few quick facts: two-thousand tons of marble were used; each column weighs fifteen and three-quarter tons, and the Legislature's cost was about $4,000,000.

Ready for a bit of trivia? How do workers change the light bulbs in the rotunda and the chamber? Those high overhead in the dome are lowered to the main floor. The maintenance staff can't do that in the Assembly with its six-hundred bulbs firmly fixed in the ceiling. In the past, workers climbed a thirty-foot scaffold, then used a long pole to unscrew the bulbs and hand them down to a fellow worker. The operation took a crew of four or five. Now, modern equipment helps to make the changes in the Assembly quicker and safer. A bucket lifts one man and a supply of bulbs within range. The changer must still use a short pole with a suction cup to reach bulbs in the crown of the ceiling.

VANDALS STRIKE

Over the years some visitors have been less than friendly and their actions have led to heavy security. At least one such visitor broke into the government power plant, determined to put out the lights at the Legislature. An Edmonton *Journal* story in July, 1939, told how an intruder wrecked the plant's four generators by pouring sand into the bearings and smashed the armatures with a sledgehammer. The lights went out in the Legislature's ground floor corridors. They would have stayed dark for an indefinite period, except for a bit of luck. The electricians discovered spare parts in storage, forgotten for thirty years. They made the repairs within a couple of days.

The incident made everyone nervous. Sabotage was a serious matter, especially with the world on the brink of another war. Tension increased when a government guard chased a prowler the following night. The police had a suspect but no one was arrested. The government ordered twenty-four hour patrols of the Legislature grounds. Security guards scoured the grounds at night with a searchlight anchored to the roof at the south end.

The Edmonton *Journal* reported, "... the beacon swung in a slow half-circle, sending a solid wall of white light on the government garage, the power plant buildings and into remote corners of the wooded grounds. It's glare could be seen all over the south side of the city and stirred widespread interest on the occasion of its Friday night debut." Certainly no place for a young man to walk his girl friend after dark.

HEAVY SECURITY

War broke out in September. Government officials guarded against any further acts of sabotage. Armed RCMP officers were on alert at the Legislature and the Administration Building to the north on 109 Street. The east and west doors of the Legislature were locked and civil servants had to produce identification cards. Police cars checked the grounds at night. Canadian Pacific had its own guards on the nearby High Level Bridge.

The most exciting incident came during one moonless night when government and railway guards were patrolling on opposite sides of a high hedge. One of the CPR guards came through an opening face to face with a rifle aimed at his chest. No shots were fired but a few choice words were exchanged.

TRAGEDY

Once the war ended, the Legislature's east and west doors were unlocked and security forces disappeared until 1956. The country was shocked by the tragic news of a mass killing of five members of the John Clark family, a hired man on their farm and a Royal Canadian Navy sailor who was visiting them for the weekend. Clark was the member for Stettler.

The police couldn't find any trace of Clark, the main suspect in the multiple-slaying. They feared he might be headed for the Legislature. A massive ground and air search came to an end more than a day later when Clark's body was found in a slough on the farm. He had shot himself.

Former Speaker Arthur Dixon of Calgary said the Clark family tragedy was one of the biggest disappointments of his time in the Assembly. He said Clark had been acting strangely, but Dixon hadn't realized that something was seriously wrong.

In the years ahead murder, suicide and death threats at the Legislature would demonstrate that being a civil servant or a politician could be a risky occupation.

The Grand Staircase.

GETTING THE PICTURE

The drone of conversation ended abruptly on the Assembly floor and in the galleries at Sergeant-at-Arms, Oscar Lacombe's command for "Order, Mr. Speaker." Carrying the mace, the symbol of parliamentary authority, he marched smartly through the main doors, leading the way for Speaker David Carter and the Assembly officials. The members stood until the Speaker offered a short prayer to open the daily sitting.

TV cameras on the side and back walls of the chamber sent the proceedings live to Edmonton's west side. Later that evening the question period was seen throughout the province on the provincial government's ACCESS TV network. ACCESS Radio broadcast the question period live on its provincial network. Other TV cameramen, radio and newspaper reporters may record the business of the Assembly. The way is open for newspaper photographers to take photographs and visitors may take notes, a break from the long British tradition forbidding the practice.

Premier Peter Lougheed's government brought the Alberta Legislature into the electronic era in 1972 - the first parliament in Canada to allow all of the media free access to the chamber. The Assembly is preparing for an even stronger electronic presence in the future. During the major renovations in 1987, cable was laid in the floor of the chamber for the addition of new equipment, when it's needed.

The main argument against TV and radio broadcast from the Assembly had been that members might lose the privilege they enjoyed to say what they wanted, leaving themselves open to possible legal action.

The danger was more political than legal. Lougheed told Premier Joey Smallwood of Newfoundland about his plans. The highly experienced Smallwood cautioned the rookie Premier, "I wouldn't do that if I were you young man." The question everyone was asking: Would the members turn into ham actors with the cameras rolling? The answer had to wait.

At the same time the members took another important step. Under the direction of Speaker Gerry Amerongen, the Assembly introduced Hansard, a printed record of the daily proceedings. Hansard is not only a service to the members but one more way for Albertans to follow what is happening.

Sergeant-at-Arms, Oscar Lacombe carries the mace into the Assembly.

"MR. SPEAKER, MR. SPEAKER"

35

SYMBOL OF AUTHORITY

Do-it-yourself Mace

Take some plumbing pipe, pieces of an old bedstead, some shaving mug handles, bits of wood, red velvet and gold paint. That's all Watson Brothers Jewellery in Calgary needed to make Alberta's first mace in 1906 at a cost of $150. The province's Liberal government placed the rush order just weeks before the first sitting of the first Alberta Legislature in 1906. Without the traditional symbol of royal authority, the provincial parliament would have been unable to meet and conduct its business.

The mace, which now represents the authority of the Speaker, dates back to medieval times when bishops carried it into battle instead of a sword. Bodyguards of King Richard 1 of England and King Philip 11 of France carried the mace and it gradually assumed a ceremonial role as a sign of the king's authority.

Now the mace is carried in front of the Speaker into the Assembly by the Sergeant-at-Arms. The mace lies on a table with the upper end pointing toward the government, signifying the Assembly is sitting. When the members sit in Committee of the Whole, a time when many of the formal rules are relaxed, the Speaker leaves his place in the chair and the mace is moved from its customary position.

Gift From Civil Servants

Alberta's original mace was supposed to be temporary but it served for fifty years. The Civil Service Association of Alberta presented the Assembly with a new mace in 1956 to mark Alberta's golden jubilee. L.B. Blain, a watchmaker and pattern-maker with Irving Kline Jewellers in Edmonton created the original design for the new mace. It was then sent to Joseph Fry Ltd. of Birmingham, England, where the firm's silversmiths took six months to complete the work.

The mace is three feet long and weighs twenty-five pounds. It contains two hundred ounces of sterling silver and is overladen with gold.

Alberta's history is part of the design. At the top is a hand-carved beaver mounted on a crown with stylized wild roses, the province's floral emblem, and sheaves of wheat. The ball of the mace has the royal coat-of-arms and the Canadian coat-of-arms.

A ring of seven gems and semi-precious stones are set around the head band of the crown. The first letter of each jewel spells the word "Alberta": Amethyst, Lapis Lazuli, Beryl, Emerald, Ruby, Topaz, and Aquamarine or Agate. On the shaft are more engraved roses and wheat sheaves, Alberta's coat-of-arms and a plaque.

The inscription reads: "The Civil Service Association of Alberta presented this mace to the people of the Province of Alberta to be held in trust by the Legislative Assembly as an expression of loyalty and in commemoration of Alberta's Golden Jubilee, 1905 - 1955."

Pages Turn

The pages pulled a few tricks of their own. The attention of the members and people in the galleries focuses on the Sergeant-at-Arms as he reverently handles the mace, the ancient symbol of authority in Commonwealth parliaments throughout the world. To drop it would be the most embarrassing of all blunders.

A group of pages in the early 1970s showed no mercy. They sprayed the mace with silicon, a slippery coating almost guaranteed to cause disaster. Sergeant-at-Arms Grant Salmon felt it slipping from his sure grasp. The tighter he gripped, the more it slipped in his hands. With the dexterity of a juggler he managed to save the mace from crashing to the floor.

Alberta's present mace was a gift from the Civil Service Association of Alberta, in celebration of the Province's golden jubilee in 1955.

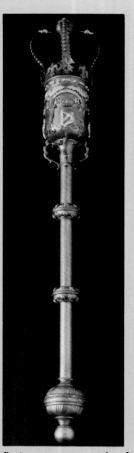

Alberta's first mace was made of scraps and spare parts.

MODERNISING THE ASSEMBLY

Alberta's lawmakers meet in a fifty-six foot square chamber, rising through the third and fourth storeys to a decorated ceiling and glass skylights. Large columns on each of the four walls support a dome over the Assembly. The public and members' galleries are on the east and west sides, the speaker's gallery on the north wall, and the press gallery behind the speaker's chair. Once the first plaster cracks were patched in 1912, little was done until 1956. Workers patched and painted the ceiling and walls, and covered them with silk to improve the acoustics and provide a suitable background for the royal portraits.

The chamber got a bright red carpet in 1970, traditionally correct for an upper house, like the Senate, but not in an Assembly. Speaker Carter suspects the hot colour raised members' tempers. Platforms were built to the right and left of the Speaker's chair for the TV cameras. Cluttered and crowded, the platforms were something of a hazard. Once a reporter stumbled as he hurried to leave the chamber and crashed to the floor. The accident interrupted Premier Lougheed, who was speaking. Hansard dutifully recorded the incident.

The makeshift platforms had other drawbacks. They hid part of the green Pennsylvania marble at the base of the columns. A curtain behind the Speaker's chair hid more marble and had become a storage area for Assembly material. Portraits of Queen Elizabeth ll and Prince Philip hung precariously on opposite walls. The time for a facelift was long overdue.

That came in 1987, as part of a major renovation to the chamber and the rotunda, under the supervision of architect Brian Woolfenden. The refurbishing of the chamber cost $845,000. Woolfenden's job was to make it a place people wanted to visit. In sharp contrast to the chamber's previous makeshift appearance, the renovations have produced a dignified and efficient meeting place. The green-grey carpet, traditional in the British House of Commons and other legislatures, turns down the emotional heat generated by debate. The subdued carpet, combined with mahogany veneer and super-white on the walls, and the beautiful mahogany desks help the television cameras produce a richer, higher quality picture.

Because all the business of the Assembly passes through the Speaker, his high-backed chair is the focal point of the chamber. It sits under a mahogany canopy, a gift of the City of Edmonton on the province's seventy-fifth anniversary. The original Canadian coat of arms on the peak of the canopy has been removed and hung in the adjoining Confederation Room, used for meetings of legislature committees. The Alberta coat of arms now decorates the peak of the canopy.

Instead of a desk for his papers and reference books, the Speaker uses two side tables with pullout boards. He has only one problem, "You can't kick off your shoes." A telephone connects him to his office, security

Top and middle: The Assembly, before and after renovations.

Below: A sound technician controls the members' microphones from this console in the Speaker's gallery.

officers at the main door and anywhere else he wants to call for assistance or information. "You've got to be prepared for everything. Eighty-three of the sharpest minds in Alberta are sitting in this room."

SECURITY GROWING CONCERN

Security has become a major concern here as it has in all parliaments in Canada. A murder-suicide in the Legislature Building in 1977, a shooting rampage in the Quebec National Assembly, and increasing threats of violence are forcing new precautions.

Alberta hasn't tightened its security as much as some Legislatures, where visitors must pass through scanning procedures common at airports. Female security guards do, however, check purses before visitors go into the galleries. No briefcases or parcels are allowed inside to eliminate the possibility of hiding weapons or explosives to throw on the Assembly floor below. Walkways behind the gallery seats have been eliminated to keep everyone in view of security guards.

Facing page, top left: The vault ceiling of the assembly features stained glass panels and six hundred light bulbs.
Top right: The stained glass in the Carillon Room was imported from Germany.
Middle: The Carillon Room still displays the old 'gingerbread house' colour scheme. The wall tapestries and stained glass ceiling add to this colourful fairy-tale look.
Bottom left: The Members' Lounge provides a relaxed atmosphere in which MLAs can discuss issues.
Bottom right: The front doors to the Assembly at the top of the Grand Staircase feature carved wild roses.

This page, top left & top right: The Speaker's suite.
Middle left: The Confederation Room is used for meetings of legislative committees.
Above: The Old Cafeteria, now used as a committee room, features stained glass ceiling panels and elegant round windows. left: MLAs can enjoy a breath of fresh air on the balcony of the Members' Lounge.

"MR. SPEAKER,
MR. SPEAKER"

VIOLENCE IN THE HALLOWED HALLS

Midnight Prowlers

Three men parked their car at the rear of the Legislature some time after midnight in late September 1960. They pried open a window and silently climbed a back stairway to the fifth floor cafeteria. They masked their faces with cloths and chose three butcher knives to use just in case there was trouble. Oscar Stephenson, the elderly night watchman, shuffled through his rounds checking doors and back rooms. The huge building with its creaks and groans was a spooky place in the middle of the night.

"Make a move and we'll kill you." Stephenson froze, he could feel the tip of the butcher knife in the small of his back. "Get down on the floor." They bound him with long roller towels and left one man to keep the knife in his back.

A few minutes later the watchman heard someone calling the janitor in the basement. The prowlers also tied him up then rushed to the office of the Edmonton Civil Service Savings and Credit Union on the fifth floor. The men wheeled the heavy safe to an elevator, loaded it into their car and disappeared. It contained $57,000 to cash pay cheques when the office opened later that morning. Stephenson freed himself forty-five minutes later and called police. The three were eventually caught and convicted.

The robbery was the second in a month at a government building. A thief slugged the manager of the cafeteria in the nearby Highways Building (later the Transportation Building), grabbed a bag with $17,000, money also meant to cash civil servants' pay cheques, and escaped. Police have no record that anyone was ever caught.

Quarrel Ends in Death

A man carrying a blue suit bag walked past the security desk at the front door of the Legislature. It was his second visit to the building that morning in October, 1977. He went directly to the third floor office of Culture Minister Horst Schmid. The minister was in hospital but Guenter Hummel wasn't paying a political call. He was looking for Victoria Breitkreuz, the girl he had hoped to marry. The two had broken up, renewed their relationship, then broke up again. She wasn't in the office when he first arrived but she was now.

When one of the secretaries saw Hummel had a rifle, she pushed a security button and ran from the office. The nervous gunman fired a shot at a security officer when he opened the outer office door but missed. A short time later there were more shots. Thirty Edmonton City Police officers and the special task force wearing bullet proof vests and carrying loaded rifles sealed off the building and entered the minister's outer office. They opened the locked door to Schmid's office. On the floor they found the secretary and the gunman, both dead, a murder-suicide.

The Legislature sat as usual that fall afternoon. Speaker Gerard Amerongen prayed for those who died during the most violent day in the Legislature's history.

MORE ELECTRONIC GADGETS

During the 1987 renovations workers prepared the chamber for the next step in the electronic revolution. Eventually, four small automated cameras mounted on the walls will replace the present ones. To get rid of the clutter on members' desks and improve the sound quality, built-in microphones have replaced the old swan-necks. Wiring is in place for desk top digital clocks, warning lights to advise members when their speaking time is up and electronic voting indicators, rather than the present system of voice and standing votes.

Frequent visitors will notice changes in the public and members' galleries. There is more seating and room for several wheelchairs. Narrower brass railings increase visibility. Twenty-two speakers in each gallery make sure the spectators don't miss a word. The next phase of improvements in the galleries will include a system to assist the hearing impaired and TV monitors to make every member visible to the visitors.

Workers raised the floor in the Speaker's Gallery, to prevent visitors from stumbling as they enter or leave. Once in the seventies, a cabinet minister's father almost tumbled over the railing to the Assembly floor below. A new addition to the gallery is a cockpit for the sound technician who controls the members' microphones. He sits at a console jutting out from the edge of the gallery. He gets a much better view than in the old position in a corner of the press gallery, which now has more room and new furniture.

The refurbishing also extended to the MLAs' lounge behind the Assembly. There, members of all parties can relax, drink coffee and talk informally. The balcony, overlooking the legislature grounds and the site of old Fort Edmonton, has patio furniture to give members a break from the windowless chamber where they work, often during the most pleasant weather of the year.

Top: Renovations to the galleries were undertaken to provide more seating and better visibility.
Left: The clock on the front of the Speaker's Gallery.

"MR. SPEAKER, MR. SPEAKER"

41

THE MEMBERS

For four years after the new Legislature was officially opened the members were all men, elected by men only. Those early Albertans heard the growing clamour for full political equality for women. Their right to vote in provincial elections was recognized on April 19, 1916. The first women to be elected to a Legislature in the British Empire took their seats in the Alberta Assembly the following year. They were nursing sister Roberta McAdams, one of the two armed services representatives, and Louise McKinney. She represented the new Non-Partisan League, a farm group.

Members in the early days of the Assembly were mostly farmers and businessmen. They quickly overcame their lack of parliamentary experience and learned the rules of the political game. Fred Kennedy, one of Alberta's early newspapermen, was impressed by the quality of legislators in 1923. "If I had expected to follow a trail of straw and hayseeds into the building, I was mistaken, because business was being transacted in quiet dignity by a group of people who appeared as if they had occupied that setting for years."

THE SPEAKER

The first act of the Assembly is to elect one of the members to fill the Office of the Speaker. The person chosen is the servant of the Assembly and must have the confidence of all members in the Assembly. His main job is to maintain order and decorum and interpret the rules of the Assembly so that the members' rights and privileges are protected. The Speaker is also a traffic cop, keeping track of the flow of paper that flows through the Assembly.

Speaker Carter sees himself "as a referee; playing in a chess game and many times in the middle of a laser light show. The experience is exhilarating. It sucks the energy right out of your bone marrow."

The Speaker can usually feel the mood of the house when he enters the Assembly and walks between the government and opposition desks. "They make comments about my hat, my walk. On days when there is no banter, look out. Something is up."

THE HOT SEAT

The highly charged question period is where the Speaker proves himself as a referee. While he has rules to guide his decisions about questions opposition and government members put to the cabinet, the Speaker can't play it strictly by the book. If he did, there would be little scope for the give and take that's part of most question periods.

"I must keep track of the questions. Are they hypothetical and therefore not allowed by the rules? Are they on the topic? In one day alone there were two points

H.C. Wilson, N.W.T.

J.F. Betts, N.W.T.

James Ross, N.W.T.

Thomas Eakins, N.W.T.

A.B. Gillis, N.W.T.

Charles Fisher

Charles Pingle

Oran McPherson

of privilege and seven points of order raised by the members. I've got to deal with all of these.''

The most contentious point of privilege Speaker Carter has dealt with so far was the use of French in the question period. He did not decide the highly sensitive issue but asked that it be referred to the twenty-one members of the Standing Committee on Privileges and Elections.

The unseen part of the Speaker's job is the administration of the Assembly office. He handles a budget of $15,000,000 and a staff of 315 people. Making decisions can result in public controversy. After Carter's first session as Speaker, the Clerk of the House, his assistant and the director of administration resigned their positions.

''I enjoy the job ninety-two per cent of the time; the other eight per cent I'm scared spitless.'' If Speaker Carter had his choice, ''Actually, I'd rather be at my forty acre retreat in the Cypress Hills at Eagle Butte.''

THE SPEAKER'S CHAIR

Seat of Authority

The nine Speakers of the Alberta Legislature have listened to thousands of hours of debate seated on three different chairs. The first was provided by the Public Works Department for Charles Fisher, the Liberal member for Banff-Cochrane, who was the Assembly's first Speaker. Following his death in 1919 during the influenza epidemic, the Assembly presented the chair to his wife. Fifty years later the family presented the chair to the Provincial Museum.

A new chair was bought for Charles Pingle, when he was named Speaker in 1920. The chair was hardly warm before Speaker Pingle lost his seat when the United Farmers of Alberta formed the new government. There was the suggestion that he should take the chair but the government decided it should stay in the Assembly.

Two succeeding Speakers, Oran McPherson and George Johnston used the chair until 1935 when Social Credit came to power. Johnston received the chair as a going-away gift. The House decided ''the chair occupied with such dignity for so many years, become the personal property of the Speaker.'' It is now in the Glenbow Museum in Calgary. It re-appeared in the Legislature in 1939 for the visit of King George VI and Queen Elizabeth.

The Public Works Department bought a new chair in 1935, which is still in use. Speaker Nathan Tanner used it for a year. The Legislature's longest serving Speaker, Peter Dawson, presided from it for twenty-five years until his death in 1963. The chair was offered to his wife but she preferred to have it used by future Speakers. It has been used by Speakers Dixon, Amerongen and Carter.

The chair has a varnished mahogany veneer with a cloth covered seat, back and arms. At the top of the high back is the provincial coat-of-arms, flanked by carved wild roses.

George Johnston

Nathan Tanner

Peter Dawson

Arthur Dixon

''MR. SPEAKER, MR. SPEAKER''

INKWELLS FLY ACROSS THE ASSEMBLY

O'Brien Hits a Nerve

The Alberta Legislature has acquired a quiet, workmanlike image. While some might call it dull, there have been characters to liven up its proceedings. Take Charles O'Brien, the first Socialist Party Member who came on the scene during construction of the new building.

The 1910 session was winding down. Premier Alexander Rutherford thought it appropriate to send condolences to the royal family on the death of King Edward Vll. O'Brien, the Member for Rocky Mountain House, didn't think much of heaping praise on the dead monarch. His education in the school of hard knocks in logging, mining and railroad camps left him hostile to the ruling elite. O'Brien's turn came after Rutherford and Opposition Leader R.B. Bennett had finished their glowing eulogies.

According to historical writer Bob Beal, O'Brien told the Assembly exactly the way he felt about royalty. "Why all this empty hypocrisy? The king was a man who worked little and ate well." He almost touched off a riot. Members started throwing inkwells and books at a ducking O'Brien. When things calmed down, he did offer an apology of sorts, which included an amendment to the motion to extend the Assembly's sympathy to the families of three hundred British miners killed in a recent disaster. No one would second the amendment so it didn't come to a vote.

After O'Brien lost his seat in 1911 he moved to the United States to become a founding member of the American Communist Party and a people's university.

The Assembly and Speaker's chair.

44

SNAKE DANCING IN THE ASSEMBLY

Socred Enthusiasm

Orvis Kennedy, the legendary Social Credit organizer and trouble shooter for Premier Ernest Manning, remembers the day well. The MLAs let their hair down so completely he doubts Alberta legislators ever will equal the frivolity of February 22, 1938.

Kennedy had just won a federal byelection called in Edmonton East to complete the term of a member of parliament who had died. The newly elected MP went to the Legislature the following day to receive the congratulations of the members. When he rose from his seat in the Speaker's gallery to acknowledge the introduction, people in the packed galleries on both sides and the fifty-six Social Credit members began to applaud. The Sergeant-at-Arms sternly announced applause was not allowed, then broke into a broad smile, "But for today, it's permitted." He joined the clapping, too.

Kennedy watched in amazement as Members suddenly snake-danced across the floor in a long weaving line. He saw Mrs. Edith Rogers, a Social Credit member, rush over and spin the chair of the Opposition Leader and try to sit on his knee. Speaker Peter Dawson didn't know what to do about the demonstration, or if he could do anything to restore order. He left his chair in the middle of the Assembly and stood in a corner. Like the amazed Orvis Kennedy, he could do nothing more than watch the Members celebrate the Social Credit victory until they were ready to return to their desks.

The Speaker's procession.

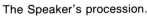

"MR. SPEAKER, MR. SPEAKER"

45

SPEAKER CHALLENGED

Arthur Dixon was another Speaker who enjoyed the job. During his term from 1963 until 1972, the Calgary member said he tried to be a "listener" to members' problems, not a "sergeant-major" to order them around. His worst moment came on a Friday afternoon during a bitter dispute between Opposition Leader Peter Lougheed and Health Minister Jim Henderson. Dixon ruled in favour of Lougheed. Henderson challenged the ruling, forcing the Assembly to decide whether to uphold his ruling. Under most circumstances the government majority would support the Speaker. Much to his dismay, the Social Credit majority voted against him. Technically he had lost the confidence of the members and should resign. Dixon waited until the following Monday before asking the members if they wanted him to quit. They said no, so he stayed.

Drawing on his experience from 1972 to 1986, the previous Speaker, Gerard Amerongen, listed several essential qualities a successful Speaker must possess. Among these: a thick hide to take criticism, especially from the media, without attempting to defend yourself publicly; above all, a good sense of humour. "It's absolutely essential. Almost any situation can be cooled with kindly humour."

Amerongen remembers one stormy question period when a Calgary Social Credit member, George Ho Lem, was criticizing the Canadian Broadcasting Corporation for showing full frontal nudity on a newscast. The Opposition member tried his best to persuade the Conservative government it should protest the CBC's breach of moral standards on the evening news. Amerongen tried to convince Ho Lem the CBC was under the jurisdiction of the federal government and not the province. He ended the member's heated attack with the quip, "No nudes is good nudes."

Former Speaker Art Dixon.

Often when members were making lengthy speeches, they took off their shoes. The temptation for other members to hide the member's shoes was just too strong to resist. Speaker Amerongen laughs about the day Gordon Stromberg, the Conservative member for Camrose, paused in the middle of his speech to complain someone had stolen his shoes.

The Speaker knew there was nothing he could do to recover the missing shoes. Instead, he warned the member of that worst of all fates for every politician, "I'm sure you're facing de-feet."

Amerongen didn't like to enforce the rule against members reading their speeches. He was convinced, that for some, reading was often far more effective. Instead of a direct rebuke to the offending member, the Speaker dispatched a page with a Herman cartoon. The cartoon read, "I liked your speech. It was the way you read it."

The former Speaker said he tried to add dignity to the office by inaugurating the more formal Speaker's procession into the Assembly through the main doors, instead of the Speaker entering the chamber alone through a side door. As an added touch of ceremony, on days dealing with government business the procession passes closest to the government desks. On opposition days, it passes closest to the opposition desks.

Amerongen also established the first intern program in Canada for university graduates who wanted to learn more about the political process. Six are chosen each year from nearly one hundred applicants to work for both the government and the opposition parties for ten months.

Left: The Alberta coat of arms is carved on the canopy above the speaker's chair.
Right: One of a speaker's many duties is to attend a number of official functions. Former speaker Gerry Amerongen is seen here with Diana, Princess of Wales.

TELEVISION GOOD OR BAD

What about the influence of television on the Assembly? Are members hamming it up? Is television looking for conflict and entertainment, then blaming the members and the Speaker's control of the proceedings when they don't materialize? By 1987, most other provincial legislatures and the House of Commons had opened their doors to TV and radio. Members are concerned the electronic media may be placing too much emphasis on the question period with its potential for political fireworks.

During his fourteen years as Speaker, Amerongen said he interpreted the rules of the question period "rather freely," allowing things to pass from both sides of the House. The proof, he said, is in Hansard. But the media and some opposition members strongly criticized his handling as too rigid, not allowing enough leeway for the opposition to question cabinet ministers.

Now, no longer the Speaker and a member of the Assembly, he can answer his critics. "Question period is nothing more than a media event. It's much more effective to stick to the business of the House and avoid personal attacks. I was constantly badgered for depriving the media of easy stories. It's easier to write up a riot."

Speaker Carter expressed some concern about what he sees as the effect of the medium that provides people with most of their news. "The legislature is much more of a media event than it used to be. There are some amateur theatrics, cases where behaviour is less sophisticated. The problem is viewers don't distinguish between Ottawa and Edmonton [The House of Commons has a reputation for much more raucous behaviour than Alberta's MLAs."]

No matter what the outcome of this debate, look for more TV coverage, not less. Former Premier Lougheed, the man who opened the Assembly's doors, is convinced television will have an even larger role to play because of its power to communicate with people directly. According to Lougheed, politicians take too seriously what newspapers say about them. "The big impact with the citizen is television."

The Legislature was a remarkable achievement for Albertans in the early 1900s. Woolfenden called the building, "A credit to the government of the day and the architect who designed it." Although no matter how well it was designed, Provincial Architect Jeffers couldn't anticipate many of today's technical demands. More restoration work is needed in the east and west wings, but the most immediate needs are for new electrical and ventilation systems. Air ducts are jammed to capacity with cable for electronic equipment. The one bright spot: new electronic equipment is getting smaller and more compact.

The "mammoth undertaking" of a pioneer age is still just that.

The Honourable David Carter, Speaker

48

VICE-REGAL ALBERTANS

Premier Peter Lougheed welcomes Her Majesty Queen Elizabeth II and His Royal Highness Prince Philip to the Legislature.

BEHIND THE GLITTER

Representing the Queen in Alberta is an exhilirating job, but for the Lieutenant-Governor, it isn't all fancy dinners, riding in a chauffeured limousine, and the pomp of the Legislature opening. Many Albertans have this image but what they don't see are the hours spent travelling the back roads, writing speeches, and the anguish some Lieutenant-Governors have endured to make tough decisions. There are days when they, like everyone else, would like nothing better than to go home and put their feet up.

Lieutenant-Governor Helen Hunley, the first woman to hold the office in Alberta, accepts about 250 engagements a year: everything from hosting the Queen Mother to visiting school children in their classrooms in Jasper. Her office works a year ahead, handling invitations on a "first come, first serve" basis.

The Lieutenant-Governor must like and enjoy meeting people. She is the province's official hostess, greeting thousands of Albertans and people from all over the world. On the advice of former Lieutenant-Governors she paces herself. "I want to live to enjoy my old age."

She works from a suite on the third floor at the north end of the Legislature. The main room is used for ceremonial occasions, like the swearing-in of members and cabinet ministers, and for the reception of special visitors. The Lieutenant-Governor's private office has her personal touch. A large banner decorates one wall, a gift from students in Jasper.

From all her many meetings with Albertans, the Lieutenant-Governor's most emotional experience was the presentation of the Order of Canada to Mrs. Ivy Taylor of Wainwright, a patient in the Wainwright Auxiliary Hospital. The 81-year-old community worker and volunteer was too sick to travel to Ottawa to receive the award personally from Governor General Jeanne Sauvé. Mrs. Taylor died a few weeks later.

Of the many organizations in which the Lieutenant-Governor is involved, she regards the Alberta Order of Excellence as one of the most important. The Legislative Assembly established the Order in 1979 to recognize the achievements of outstanding Albertans. As its Chancellor, she presides at the annual investiture ceremony. Each new member receives a silver medallion and a lapel badge. Four outstanding Albertans were honoured in 1986, bringing the total number of members in the Order to fifteen.

Left, top to bottom: Joseph Royal, N.W.T.; M.C. Cameron, N.W.T.; Edgar Dewdney, N.W.T.; C.H. McIntosh, N.W.T.
Mid-left, top: A.E. Forget, N.W.T.
Mid-left, bottom: David Laird, N.W.T.
Mid-right: G.H.V. Bulyea
Right: Dr. George Brett

OTTAWA CONNECTION

In the province's early days, the Lieutenant-Governor was an agent of the federal government, expected to advise the province about the intent of federal legislation and ensure provincial laws were in line with federal legislation. Alberta's first Lieutenant-Governor, George Bulyea, a former Liberal politician in the old Northwest Territories government, understood that role well. When Alexander Rutherford became entangled in the railway scandal and no longer had the confidence of federal Liberals, Bulyea moved quickly to secure his resignation and choose a successor.

Ernest Watkins wrote about Bulyea, ''Judging by his actions, his role as he saw it was to act as the representative in Alberta of the Liberal government in office in Ottawa and to protect their interests as best he could.''

EARLY LIEUTENANT-GOVERNORS

Four Albertans served as Lieutenant-Governors in the next two decades. Dr. Robert Brett, who pioneered the development of the Banff Hot Springs, held the office from 1915 to 1927. His achievements in bringing relief to the sick through the Banff sanitarium received worldwide recognition.

A 1906 publication, ''Souvenir of Alberta,'' speaks glowingly of Dr. Brett. ''The force of the aphorism which bids us seize opportunity by the forelock, has had a striking illustration in the career of Dr. Robert G. Brett, founder and proprietor of the celebrated sanitarium at Banff, the praises of which are sounded by men and women who have received its benefits in almost every part of the civilized world.''

Another physician, Dr. William Egbert of Calgary succeeded Brett. He served from 1927 to 1931. A Calgary lawyer, William Walsh, was the next office holder, from 1931 to 1936. Philip Primrose, a soldier, a member of the North West Mounted Police and a magistrate was appointed in 1936, only to die after just six months in office.

REFUSED TO SIGN

The best example of a direct challenge by a Lieutenant-Governor to the provincial government came in 1937 when John Campbell Bowen, a Baptist minister and former Liberal member and Leader of the Opposition, refused to sign three pieces of legislation passed by Premier William Aberhart's Social Credit government. Two of the bills involved matters under federal jurisdiction, and the third was a move to stifle the press.

Ernest Manning was a cabinet minister and close to the crisis that day in October. ''I don't know how wise it was for Bowen not to sign the bills. It was a unique situation.'' The future Premier said the Lieutenant-Governor should have signed and let the courts decide.

Bowen's action so infuriated Aberhart that it cost Attorney General John Hugill his job because he sided with Bowen. The following year the Socreds closed Government House, the gracious sandstone mansion overlooking the river valley in Edmonton's west end, that was the Lieutenant-Governor's official residence. Was the provincial government hitting back? Senator Manning denied there was any personal retaliation against Bowen. The decision to close Government House was ''economic,'' a casualty of the Depression.

While Government House was no longer home for Lieutenant-Governor Bowen and his successors, they weren't on the street. They now live in a smaller residence about a mile west of Government House, more suited to today's less pretentious lifestyle.

Left: Dr. William Egbert
Mid-left: William Walsh
Mid-right, top: Philip Primrose
Mid-right, bottom: John Bowlen
Right, top to bottom: John C. Bowen; J. Percy Page;
Grant MacEwan; Ralph Steinhauer

THE OLD GREY LADY

High Living

Six of Alberta's twelve Lieutenant-Governors lived in luxury in the great sandstone mansion on the rim of the valley at 128th Street and 102nd Avenue, within sight of the Legislature Building. Nothing in the province could match the residence, its landscaped grounds and spectacular view of the winding North Saskatchewan River. Lieutenant-Governor George Bulyea officially opened the opulent mansion which cost $345,000 in 1913.

Less than three decades later, the house was shut tight, a casualty of hard times; a bitter dispute between Premier William Aberhart and Lieutenant-Governor John Bowen a few months before didn't help. The residence had narrowly escaped closure at the hands of the United Farmers of Alberta government in 1925.

Second World War pilots and disabled veterans called it home. It was sold to the federal government and its furnishings auctioned, bought back and by 1967 started a new life as a conference centre. In 1975 the Progressive Conservatives began the restoration of the old house at a cost of $1.7 million, five times its original price tag.

Even More Gorgeous

Two rooms survived from the high-stepping carriage days, the governor's library and an upstairs bedroom. The rest of the house was converted into meeting, entertaining and dining facilities, a showplace fit for world leaders. The eye-catcher is the third-floor Alberta Room, a conference room with space for 79 participants and almost perfect acoustics. A feature to note is the domed ceiling with suspended plaster petals shaped like a daisy, which appear to float because of the effect of indirect lighting.

The building needed extensive structural changes. Steel trusses were installed to support the sagging roof. Stonemasons built a new west wall to enclose a staircase because of fire regulations. While the interior of Government House has changed drastically, officials tried to preserve as much of the original quality workmanship as possible. One of the oddest features, a half-inch of horsehair under the floors, presumably to prevent squeaking, disappeared in the renovations.

The ''old grey lady,'' a name from its earlier era, now works seven days a week, providing a place for people who come to talk and others who come just to look at something of what the Lieutenant-Governors' residence once was.

ALBERTA'S FIRST LIEUTENANT-GOVERNOR

Powerful Figure

When George Hedley Vicars Bulyea stepped forward to take the oath of office as Alberta's first Lieutenant-Governor on September 1, 1905, it was the high point of his involvement with government in the developing west. For the next ten years he would be a power in the political life of the young province.

George Bulyea was born in Gagetown, New Brunswick. He graduated at the head of his class in Mathematics and French at the University of New Brunswick in 1878. He came to the west four years later after a brief teaching stint.

Bulyea settled in Qu'Appelle and established a business dealing in furniture, and flour and feed. Twelve years later he was elected to the Council of the Northwest Territories at Regina. Bulyea held several major cabinet posts: Minister of Agriculture, Provincial Secretary, and Minister of Public Works. He was a Liberal, which put him in a good position when Prime Minister Sir Wilfrid Laurier was making the key appointments of Lieutenant-Governor and Premier to launch the new province.

Bulyea served a second term as the Lieutenant-Governor and saw both the Legislature Building and Government House completed and officially opened. They were mighty symbols of the new political reality on the western prairies. He left office in 1915 and became the chairman of the Public Utilities Commission. Bulyea died in 1928.

Government House in 1929. The late Sir Winston Churchill is at the far right.

POST WAR ERA

John Bowlen, a rancher from Calgary and Liberal member for fourteen years in the Legislature, was appointed Lieutenant-Governor in 1950 at the age of seventy-four. He was one of the six opposition members who survived the Social Credit landslide in 1935. Although they were from different generations and divided by politics, Bowlen and Premier Ernest Manning became close friends.

During debate in the House, Bowlen often attacked Manning over some government policy, then sent him a note, "Don't pay any attention to what I said." Once any confrontation between the two in the Assembly had finished, they would join each other for a cup of tea in the cafeteria. Bowlen accepted a second term as Lieutenant-Governor but he died in 1959 before completing it. He is buried in Edmonton.

His successor was a world famous basketball coach, J. Percy Page. He completed Bowlen's term and served a full term of his own. The phenomenal success he enjoyed as coach of 'The Grads', the Commercial Graduates Basketball Club far outshadowed his political career, as a member of the Legislature and Lieutenant-Governor.

Page had been a teacher and principal at McDougall Commercial High School in Edmonton. His teams completely dominated women's basketball throughout the world from 1915 to 1940. They won ninety-three per cent of their games and forty-nine Canadian championships.

A NEW SPIRIT

With the appointment of J.W. Grant MacEwan in 1966, Albertans soon detected a more relaxed, much less formal approach to the office of Lieutenant-Governor. The university professor, historian, author and politician travelled the province challenging students and Albertans of all ages to strive for excellence in everything they set out to do.

Don Cunningham, an elevator operator at the Legislature, noticed the different approach soon after MacEwan took office. The veteran of the Second World War watched five Lieutenant-Governors come and go from his elevator on the east side of the Legislature rotunda. "Page was all protocol. MacEwan was eighteen thousand miles away from protocol." Cunningham laughed about the day he saw the Lieutenant-Governor rushing across the rotunda to catch the elevator. "MacEwan was carrying a garden rake he had bought on sale at a downtown department store at noon."

The tall, affable Lieutenant-Governor reached out to Albertans in a way no other person in that office had done. He was a familiar figure striding along with a group of young people in 'Miles for Millions' marches. They were twenty-six mile walks first organized by Dr. William Liston, an Edmonton radiologist, and his wife Ruth, to raise funds for Oxfam's Third World projects.

The Lieutenant-Governor started early and always was among the early finishers.

Above: His Honour, the Honourable John J. Bowlen, Lieutenant-Governor of Alberta, 1950-1959.

Right: Still active today, Grant MacEwan is seen here helping a group of young Albertans plant a tree in celebration of Forestry Week.

NATIVE PEOPLE HONOURED

Another first was the appointment of Ralph Steinhauer of the Saddle Lake Indian Reserve near St. Paul, a full treaty Indian of the Cree tribe and great grandson of the famous western missionary, Henry Bird Steinhauer. He had more than three decades of experience as a band councillor and chief, and was one of the founders of the Indian Association of Alberta. Albertans welcomed his choice as the Lieutenant-Governor, but Steinhauer was unsure what the reaction would be from other tribes in the province.

After much discussion with his wife Isabel, "We decided to take the plunge." To their relief the reaction from other treaty Indians and everyone else was "tremendously favourable." So favourable that the Kainai Chiefs, a Blood Indian organization in Southern Alberta, inducted him into their select group which includes Prime Ministers and other distinguished Canadians. The Lieutenant-Governor's Kainai name - Sitting Eagle.

The opening of the Legislature in 1977 was a day of great pride for native people throughout the province. Steinhauer read the Speech from the Throne in his full Indian regalia, including his headdress, to mark the centennial of the signing of Treaties Six and Seven. These agreements between the Indian tribes and Queen Victoria provided the land for much of the new province.

That day dreaded by all Lieutenant-Governors came for Steinhauer. That's the day they must consider refusing to sign legislation passed by the legislature. He was under pressure from native groups to delay a bill dealing with disputed land in the Fort McMurray area. The Lieutenant-Governor met with Premier Peter Lougheed, a land claims official, and others to help him make a decision. With the best advice available, he concluded: if the legislation was within the power of the provincial legislature, he had to sign. It was and he did.

BACK FENCE ROMANCE

"The cowboy is following the Indian," was Frank Lynch-Staunton's comment at a banquet to honour the outgoing Lieutenant-Governor and to formally introduce himself as Steinhauer's successor. Their lives had followed similar patterns. Both men were born in the year Alberta became a province, both were men of the land; Steinhauer a farmer, Lynch-Staunton a rancher.

During his term from 1979 to 1983, the new Lieutenant-Governor kept a picture of a tough looking old cowhand over the fireplace. The caption read, "There were a hell of a lot of things they didn't tell me when I signed on with this outfit." The caption touched a chord with many people who saw it. Premier Peter Lougheed came into the Lieutenant-Governor's office one day, glanced at the picture and agreed with the sentiment: "There were a hell of a lot of things they didn't tell me either."

Alberta's eleventh Lieutenant-Governor brought a touch of romance to the office. He carried on an over-the-back-fence courtship few people knew about until he married Muriel Shaw, a woman he first met in university. She lived next door to his official residence. "It was convenient," he laughed.

Lynch-Staunton agreed with other Lieutenant-Governors that the people he met made the job. However, he discovered another side to the formalities, that was not all that enjoyable. He candidly admitted that he found the repitition of so many banquets boring. "You were on display. I didn't like that. You were always expected to say a few words and I'm no orator." For the cowboy, one term was enough.

A remark, for which Lynch-Staunton will long be remembered, came late one fall evening after he prorogued the Legislature. Once the formalities were complete, he told the members the price he had paid to let them get away that night rather than the following day. The Lieutenant-Governor had been enjoying himself at a reception, one he was reluctant to leave. "I left a hell of a party to come down here."

FIRST WOMAN

Just how much the office of Lieutenant-Governor has changed became apparent on January 22, 1985. Helen Hunley was installed as Alberta's twelfth Lieutenant-Governor, but, far more importantly, she was the first woman to be so honoured.

She brought to the job a background of service and experience gained in the rough and tumble of the business world. During World War Two, she was a member of the Canadian Women's Army Corps, with two years of overseas service. She was a councillor and Mayor of Rocky Mountain House, involved in community groups, a Progressive Conservative member of the Legislature and a cabinet minister for eight years.

Men sometimes call Miss Hunley 'His Honour'; old habits are hard to break. She doesn't expect to be treated any differently as a woman in the province's highest office. She does, however, feel a certain compulsion to do well because she is a woman. Certain things take more time. "There's more fussing over your clothes and hair."

VICE-
REGAL
ALBERTANS

55

The Lieutenant-Governor glances over her shoulder once in a while hoping she won't have to face the crisis John Bowen faced in 1937. To avoid such situations, Premier Don Getty and government officials fully explain the import of all government documents she is expected to sign. The fact that a woman's signature is there at all would be proof enough to Lieutenant-Governor George Bulyea that his political era, one in which women didn't have the vote or the right to sit in the Legislature, has disappeared.

Below: Her Honour the Lieutenant-Governor of Alberta, Helen Hunley, reviewing an all-woman honour guard.

Left:
The Honourable Helen Hunley reads the Speech from the Throne at the opening of the Legislature.

BEHIND THE PREMIER'S DESK

THE SEIGE

William Aberhart slumped in his chair in the premier's office. Everything had gone wrong when it should have been going right. Less than two years before, his Social Credit party had crushed its opposition, winning fifty-six of sixty-three seats. Now a group of insurgents, hand-picked Social Credit members, were demanding his resignation. They accused him of taking too long to introduce Social Credit in the Depression-weary province.

His latest budget, which raised taxes, infuriated them. Aberhart had no choice, the province was bankrupt and civil servants' pay cheques were bouncing at the banks. The budget debate attracted twelve hundred people. They jammed the galleries and the overflow crowded the hallways to listen on loudspeakers. They heard Aberhart's own members call him names. They demanded "men … who can stand before a demagogue and damn his treacherous flatteries."

The Socred caucus had kicked out Aberhart and his ministers so they could lambaste them without any need to hold back. At times, Alfred Hooke, the chairman, almost lost control of the meeting. Emotions ran so high some members got sick and left the room. "They came close to fist fights."

Finally at one in the morning, the Premier and his ministers returned to the caucus. "They looked like whipped men," Hooke said recalling that March night in 1937. "We weren't trying to get rid of Aberhart. We wanted to save him." Aberhart made a deal: Give him enough to pay the government's bills for three months. In return, Albertans would get the promised $25 dividend and he would move on other measures

to implement Social Credit. The insurgents agreed, ending the crisis. The premier's office was Aberhart's until his death in 1943.

The Aberhart years are among the most fascinating in the province's political history. No other Alberta Premier has suffered such severe attacks and survived, although each of the eleven from Alexander Rutherford to Don Getty have faced their own crises. For ten of them the third floor east wing marked "Office of the Premier" has been a haven, a place to re-group and move ahead or move out.

That inner sanctum is a large panelled room with a fireplace at the far end. The furnishings are ordinary but comfortable. No one is sure whether the premier's desk came with Premier Arthur Sifton, the first occupant. The room has changed little since then. The occasional new rug has been the only expense. Premier Manning didn't think it was right to spend the money, but a new rug mysteriously appeared in the late 1950s, while he was away on a business trip.

POLITICAL LIABILITY

Alberta's first Premier, Alexander Rutherford, quickly discovered how mean and unfair politics could be. He lead the Liberals to two overwhelming victories but saw it all disappear when his government became emmeshed in a railway scandal. The provincial Liberals were badly split. Twelve of Rutherford's members voted against him. In the eyes of federal Liberals, the Premier was a political liability. Rutherford resigned and lost the chance to put his feet on the premier's desk in the magnificent new Legislature.

The Honourable Alexander Cameron Rutherford, Alberta's first premier (1905-1913).

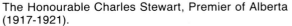

The Honourable Charles Stewart, Premier of Alberta (1917-1921).

The Honourable Arthur Sifton, Premier of Alberta (1913-1917).

His successor was Arthur Sifton, the Chief Justice of Alberta. Ernest Watkins later wrote that he doubted any convention would have elected Sifton leader. "Instead he had many of the qualities of a professional soldier, a general. He liked order, discipline and obedience." R.B. Bennett, the future Prime Minister, nicknamed Sifton "the Czar."

Sifton, the first Premier to occupy the third floor office, had little time to enjoy his new surroundings. His government was short of cash to pay the construction bills, so he sent a five-man posse to three banks to collect money he claimed rightfully should be in the provincial treasury. The posse returned empty handed. Sifton took the dispute all the way to the Privy Council in London and lost - a 'wastebasket-kicking day' in the premier's office when the news broke. He will best be remembered for eight years of prohibition in the province, from 1915 to 1923.

When Sifton resigned in 1917 to run as a federal candidate, the Liberals chose Charles Stewart, a farmer, to be the next occupant of the premier's office. Stewart couldn't cope with falling grain prices and a slumping economy, so the province's voters deserted the Liberals for the United Farmers of Alberta in the 1921 election.

MEET MR. SOCIAL CREDIT

Trouble in Rocky

Alfred J. Hooke, a former Social Credit cabinet minister and deputy premier, closely observed William Aberhart, the founder of the Alberta Social Credit Movement. "Aberhart was an organizer with boundless energy and great ability to motivate people." A small group of bar flies in Hooke's constituency of Rocky Mountain House learned first-hand just how well Aberhart could handle troublemakers. They decided it would be great sport to disrupt one of his meetings. Their enthusiasm grew with each round of beer. Hooke heard about the plan and alerted Aberhart. The hecklers planned to sit in the back row of the meeting hall, but when Aberhart arrived he insisted they sit in the first row.

The hecklers didn't say a word during the meeting. At the conclusion of his speech, Aberhart invited the ringleader to share the platform and give the crowd his solution to Alberta's economic problems. The red-faced man declined. The two shook hands and Social Credit had won another supporter.

Front and reverse sides of a Social Credit Prosperity Certificate.

Mind Benders

Orvis Kennedy, an Edmonton hardware merchant and Social Credit organizer, often travelled with Aberhart throughout the province. Rather than spend endless hours making small talk, Aberhart used the time to exercise their minds. "Rolling stones gather no moss. Why?" The discussion was underway.

On one trip, Kennedy criticized the popular slogan used by one of the radio soap operas of the day. He said "Whiter than white" was misleading and shouldn't be used. How could anything be whiter than white?

Aberhart invariably took the opposing side of an argument. He used the Bible to prove his case. "Everything is relative. When you die and go to heaven, the Bible says you will wear white. It will definitely be whiter than any white clothing you wore on earth. In fact, your earthly white will look positively tattletale grey. See, everything is relative."

Cruelest Cut

When Aberhart's political opponents couldn't win on the platform, they sometimes tried to even scores in the parking lot. Kennedy used his own car to transport Aberhart from meeting to meeting. More than once vandals dumped sugar into his gas tank, or stole his briefcase and rifled his papers

Aberhart ignored the abuse, but he wasn't prepared for a stinging rebuke from the Board of Governors at the University of Alberta. A representative of the board told him informally that the institution planned to confer a Doctorate of Laws degree on him for his contributions to education in the province. The premier was elated by the news and began preparing notes for a convocation address. Soon after, he was informed the selection committee had rejected him and the board witheld the degree.

Left: The Honourable Robert Greenfield, Premier of Alberta (1921-1925).
Above: Greenfield at home on his farm (1924).

FARMERS TAKE OVER

The UFA was a farmers' movement and didn't have a political leader. They couldn't make up their minds who should be the next Premier. Henry Wise Wood, the president, refused the job. The party choose Robert Greenfield, a Peace River farmer. He found it tough sitting behind the premier's desk, grappling with government administration and trying to produce effective policies. By 1925, he was packing his briefcase. Greenfield's own members turned against him in the legislature and he resigned.

As John Brownlee, a lawyer, settled in, Albertans were getting their first case of oil fever. The Turner Valley field near Calgary was producing oil and huge quantities of natural gas. Unfortunately, there was no market for the gas. Brownlee decided it was time to act on an old federal problem to ensure Alberta shared in any future oil boom. He pressured Prime Minister Mackenzie King's shaky minority government to transfer the control of natural resources and crown lands to the Alberta government. In a desperate bid to gain political support in the west, King agreed to the transfer in 1930. Brownlee and his ministers were jubilant. It was like winning all the lotteries in the world.

The celebration was short-lived. The Depression capped the oil boom for seventeen years. Alberta's treasury looked like four flats on a Model T. Brownlee had enough to handle with news pouring across his desk of the latest economic disaster and the growing fascination of Alberta farmers with Social Credit. The last thing he needed was screaming headlines about his personal life.

SCANDAL DESTROYS PREMIER

The story hit the front pages when a young woman from Edson and her father filed a civil suit against him for seduction. Vivian MacMillan was a secretary in the Attorney General's department. She claimed the Premier had persuaded her to work in Edmonton, that she became his mistress, and that they had sex on numerous occasions.

When the case went to court in the spring of 1934 the province's newspapers carried every claim and denial for five days. The jury awarded the girl $10,000 and her father, a railway employee, $5,000. In a strange twist, the trial judge disagreed with the verdict and refused to enter the judgment. The Supreme Court of Canada eventually awarded the MacMillans the original damages. On the day following the trial, Brownlee announced his resignation as Premier.

The UFA caucus took three days to choose Richard Gavin Reid, a veteran cabinet minister, as his successor. By the time Reid called an election a year later the province's farmers had jumped to Social Credit. Not one UFA candidate survived the onslaught. Senator Ernest Manning, then a newly-elected Socred, remembered his first trip to the Legislature with Premier Aberhart for a meeting with the outgoing Premier to discuss the changeover. "It was a cool meeting. Reid was very bitter about his government's defeat."

The defeated Premier had every right to be bitter. Even in his own district of Mannville, east of Edmonton, where he had been a pioneer homesteader, people turned against him. Reid discovered that only three of his eighteen relatives in the area, eligible to vote, had voted for him. The rest supported Social Credit. The bitterness over his defeat certainly didn't affect his health. Reid worked until he was ninety-five and died when he was one hundred and one.

The Honourable John E. Brownlee, Premier of Alberta (1925-1934).

THE MANNING YEARS

Aberhart's sudden death in Vancouver in 1943 shocked the party. The caucus chose as a successor the young Ernest Manning, then only thirty-four, and an associate of Aberhart's from the early days at the Prophetic Bible Institute in Calgary. Manning managed the province's affairs for the next twenty-five years until his retirement in 1968.

The young Premier made one last unsuccessful attempt to implement Social Credit. The legislature passed a two-part Bill of Rights, declaring the inalienable right of every citizen to enjoy his property and to exercise his civil rights. The second part outlined the means to put those rights into practice. However, the Judicial Committee of the Privy Council in London declared the attempt beyond the powers of the province, a familiar story for Socreds trying to change the monetary system.

Manning's main political target became what he saw as the socialist threat in the rise of the CCF party. While he liked to tell reporters he enjoyed administration more than politics, no one could match his political skills. Much of that success was due to his ability to anticipate people's needs.

The Honourable Richard Gavin Reid, Premier of Alberta (1934-1935).

The Honourable William Aberhart, Premier of Alberta (1935-1943).

The Honourable Ernest C. Manning, Premier of Alberta (1943-1968).

Left: The Executive Council Chamber, where cabinet meetings are held.

BEHIND THE PREMIER'S DESK

IN TOUCH WITH PEOPLE

On a trip through northern Alberta, Manning met with local doctors to find out the health needs of the area. Out of that meeting came free maternity care for all Alberta mothers and their newborn children. Reporter Fred Kennedy put it succinctly, "There is no one like Manning to keep grass [the grassroots] in touch with brass."

The discovery of oil in Leduc in 1947 helped to bankroll Manning's five-year social programs, the key to his success at the polls. On one occasion, he misread the desires of the voters. The Socreds decided to pay Albertans dividends from the oil revenues. The payments of $20 and $17.50 over two years got a mixed reaction, especially when reports surfaced of people collecting far more than what they were entitled to. A government survey showed sixty per cent of the people wanted the money used to build senior citizens' lodges. Manning discontinued the dividends and announced the construction of fifty lodges, the cornerstone of his next election campaign.

Although the Premier was a big spender on education and other services, he took a hard second look at requests to spend much smaller amounts. Soon after the MLAs received a $500 raise to $5,300 a year, in 1967, Dr. Walter Buck, the member for Clover Bar, tried to convince the caucus that members from remote areas should get four free air trips a year. Manning told the freshman Socred member, "When you're spending your own money, do anything you like. When you're spending the taxpayer's money, it's a sacred trust. You can't do things like that."

HOOKE'S ENTERTAINERS

Even with the new oil money, Manning's approach to spending forced Alf Hooke, by then a cabinet minister, to organize a group of volunteer entertainers 'The Westerners' to raise money for regional libraries. The government still couldn't find enough money to pay library grants. Hooke's comic songs were a big hit in rural Alberta. He even spent $800 out of his own pocket to buy a bus to transport the group. The Westerners continued to tour for ten years.

Many Albertans had the impression Manning made all the major decisions for his cabinet ministers. Ray Speaker contends it was just the opposite. "He told ministers they had a job to do and left them alone."

Sometimes during their cabinet meetings the ministers could hear voices from the opposition offices below coming through the heating ducts. To make sure secrets weren't leaking the cabinet ordered several checks for hidden bugs but no devices were found. Speaker said the only cabinet leaks were sitting around the table. A couple of ministers couldn't keep anything confidential. They spilled everything to reporters soon after the cabinet meetings ended.

Dr. Buck was impressed with Manning's openness. The Premier told his members not to vote for measures they couldn't support. When the government introduced legislation to allow dental mechanics to fit dentures, Dr. Buck, who was a dentist, was free to vote as he wished. There was no criticism from the Premier that he had broken party unity.

Manning demonstrated even greater flexibility on the question of slow relaxation of the province's liquor laws. He allowed a free vote in the Assembly on a motion to introduce mixed drinking in the major cities, despite his own firm opposition. Because of his weekly Bible broadcasts, many Albertans thought Manning was opposed on religious grounds. His conviction stemmed from what he saw as the tragic consequences of drinking. "It's a stupid thing to do."

NEW MAN IN THE OFFICE

The Socreds held their first leadership convention when Manning retired in 1968. There was no darker horse than Dr. Buck, who ran as a youth candidate. He was thirty-seven and had been an MLA for only a year. His candidacy demonstrated the desire for change in a party that had been in power for thirty-two years. "I was Premier for 10 seconds when they announced the results of the final ballot because of the alphabetical order of the candidates," Buck laughed. He ran third to Harry Strom and Gordon Taylor.

Young Socreds looked to the new Premier to reform and energize the party. Strom, a successful farmer and sixteen year veteran of Manning cabinets, was open to change but couldn't deliver it. He was in much the same position Reid had been in 1935 after taking over from a strong leader and facing the challenge of a dynamic new political opponent. In Strom's case it was Peter Lougheed.

Albertans were waiting for Strom to test his leadership at the polls. In July 1971, he climbed off the horse he had ridden in Edmonton's annual Klondike Days Parade, returned to his office and called an election for August 30. For Strom, it was a ride into political oblivion.

The Honourable Harry Strom, Premier of Alberta (1968-1971).

THE LEGISLATURE'S
MOST TERRIFYING DAY

Facing the Mob

Premier Harry Strom and his Social Credit members knew they were in trouble when live chickens and eggs began to fall with a splat from the fifth floor of the rotunda. At least a thousand angry farmers had stormed through the front door of the Legislature. Another thousand were demonstrating outside that day in the late 1960s. They were upset by a rumour the government was planning to increase the fuel oil tax. Ray Speaker, the acting Minister of Agriculture, blamed the Progressive Conservative Opposition for spreading the rumour.

Inside the Assembly the members squirmed every time they heard the demonstrators yell, ''We want Strom.'' When the Premier failed to appear, the farmers suddenly began to chant, ''Break it down. Break it down.'' They were carrying a battering ram to smash the main doors of the Assembly. Strom signalled to Speaker and another cabinet minister, Bob Clark, to follow him into the hallway to meet the demonstrators.

The three worked their way through the shouting farmers. Speaker spotted the leader of the group, standing near the main entrance. Speaker promised Strom would meet with a small group of representatives. ''But for heaven's sake, calm down before someone gets hurt or the building comes down.'' In his office, the Premier assured the farmers the government had no intention of raising the fuel oil tax, despite what they might have been told. The leaders, in turn, convinced the distraught farmers in the hallways the rumour was untrue. The crisis was over.

More Protests

As the province moved into the 1970s, more groups and individuals demonstrated in front of the Legislature. Usually they voiced their concerns, then left. However, the Piches, an Indian family from northern Alberta, wanted to erect a tipi on the Legislature grounds. They were trying to draw attention to the racial discrimination and poverty endured by most native people in northern Alberta. The Edmonton City Police had forcibly removed their tipi from the grounds in front of City Hall. When they moved to the Legislature grounds, police and security guards were ready, once again, to remove them.

Deputy Premier Anders Aalborg believed the Piches should have an opportunity to speak out for the poor in Alberta society. He persuaded his colleagues to overrule the police and to allow the family to erect their tipi, no matter how embarrassing their presence might be for the Alberta government. After the cabinet meeting Aalborg said the police reaction had been ''overenthusiastic.''

Above: Angry farmers protest the Strom government (April 1, 1970).

TEAM TORY TAKES OVER

Peter Lougheed and his Progressive Conservatives won forty-nine seats with an image of energy and just enough change. In Senator Manning's view, the Conservative victory wasn't so much a rejection of Social Credit, rather the feeling that Albertans wanted something new and younger leaders. Both political parties had much the same approach. ''It was like buying a different car model from General Motors.''

Soon after Peter Lougheed settled in, he converted the third floor of the east wing into a personal compound, the centre of government activity. His own private office remained much the same, preserving the atmosphere and tradition of its former occupants. A small room, seldom used by former premiers, connected his office with a balcony over the east entrance to the Legislature. Lougheed converted it into ''the patio,'' a place to enjoy lunch on a warm summer day.

At least one major government decision, the purchase of Pacific Western Airlines, was made there. Don Getty said the code name for the highly secret transaction was the 'patio project'. Lougheed, Getty and the others involved were quickly tagged the 'patio crowd'.

Below: The Premier's Office is located in the east wing.
Right: Each marble column weighs fifteen and three-quarter tons.
Bottom right: The Office of the Premier.

The hallway outside the premier's office was now blocked off. In the past, reporters had wiled away the time there waiting for news conferences by throwing pennies against the wall to see who could come closest. The hallway and adjoining rooms were converted to offices for a growing staff of assistants. The cabinet room across the hall doubled as a news conference centre to meet the demands of a much larger press gallery. Even a public washroom was renovated and turned into an office for Lougheed's press secretary and an assistant.

The Premier maintained his personal contact with Albertans through cabinet tours around the province

Above: Premier Aberhart and his wife welcome His Majesty King George VI and Queen Elizabeth (May, 1939).
Below: Premier Lougheed greets Queen Elizabeth, the Queen Mother (1983).

- "Getting out from under the dome," he called the forays. In one small community the Premier stepped from his helicopter and rushed over to greet a group of children. As he put out his hand, the excited youngsters rushed past him without stopping, eager to get a closer look at the chopper.

BEHIND THE PREMIER'S DESK

THE BOOM YEARS

Alberta rushed into the seventies with Lougheed fully in control and ready to take on the federal government mainly over energy and the constitution. The province was awash in oil and natural gas money, which allowed his government to establish the Heritage Savings and Trust Fund and a wide range of social programs. He had planned to stay in office for two terms. Instead, he stayed to fight through four elections, mainly because of what he saw as the threat posed by Prime Minister Pierre Trudeau and the federal Liberals.

Lougheed's toughest decision came in the fall of 1980, in response to the federal government's National Energy Program. The Premier and his ministers saw the program as a political powerplay. Alberta threatened to turn down the oil taps and reduce shipments to eastern Canada, unless Trudeau changed provisions in the federal budget which could harm Alberta's economy. "It worked. It was the hardest decision I ever made, because I'm a Canadian before an Albertan and I expected a backlash."

Lougheed prides himself that his government's policy on major issues was set by the caucus. Did he ever overrule the members? "Never, never. But I certainly was forceful on subjects I thought were fundamental." Cabinet meetings were different. He sometimes got his way no matter what his ministers had decided. Lougheed used to tell the story of how he had lost a cabinet vote by seventeen to one on some issue. "I just barely managed to get it through."

One of the best politicians of the Lougheed era was Deputy Premier Dr. Hugh Horner from Barrhead. Even his strongest opponents, like Dr. Walter Buck, admired his skills. "He understood rural people. If you wanted something done, go to Horner." Dr. Buck attributed much of Lougheed's success to the Member for Barrhead.

GETTY RETURNS

Don Getty, the Edmonton Eskimo football quarterback, an oilman, and one of the six original Tories, didn't want a cabinet job in 1971. Four years later he was ready to quit politics and was only persuaded by Lougheed to stay for another four year term. Getty didn't like the drudgery of administration. He had seen too many Social Credit cabinet ministers carrying stacks of files into the chamber to read and sign while debates were underway. Getty feared cabinet responsibilities would interfere with his family life. Lougheed allowed him to leave cabinet meetings early to watch his son play football. "My family comes first."

His eight years as a cabinet minister and four in the Official Opposition gave him the political experience to succeed Peter Lougheed in 1986. He was directly involved in the government purchase of Pacific Western Airlines. It was Getty who first suggested to Lougheed that they buy the airline to prevent British Columbia from taking over Alberta's traditional role as the supplier of the north.

The Alberta Energy Company, a mix of government and private ownership, was conceived by Getty during a holiday in Hawaii. Many of Alberta's small investors had told him they felt shut out of investing in the oil industry, that they weren't a part of it. Getty piloted the idea through cabinet and the company was born.

The future Premier learned a lot about tough negotiating in the formation of Syncrude in the mid-seventies. At one tense meeting with the oil company representatives, Getty slammed his files shut and started to walk out. His abrupt action changed the mood of the negotiators. An oil company representative grabbed his arm and asked him not to leave. "They talked us into it instead of us talking them into a deal."

The Honourable Peter Lougheed, Premier of Alberta (1971-1986).

GETTY STYLE

The Premier's style of government is different from Peter Lougheed's. "Lougheed was intense. It was his party." Getty's style is more relaxed. He plans to give responsibility to his ministers for a period of time, evaluate their performance then, if necessary, make changes. Getty doesn't get defensive about Tory members speaking their minds in public, even when their views differ with government policy.

The success of Getty's time in the premier's office will depend largely on how he handles the province's economy, the same crucial problem practically all of Alberta's premiers have faced since 1905.

Premier Don Getty shakes hands with New Democrat member Bob Hawksworth.

PREMIER WHO?

Et tu Getty?
Peter Lougheed rushed on ahead through the tunnel connecting the Chateau Laurier Hotel in Ottawa with the National Conference Centre. He was a freshman Premier eager to participate in his first meeting with Prime Minister Pierre Trudeau and the other Premiers. In his rush he forgot his security pass.

A few moments later, Don Getty, the Minister of Federal and Intergovernmental Affairs and a close associate since their days in opposition, arrived at the entrance to the centre wearing his pass. A security man approached him, "That fellow over there says he's the Premier of Alberta. And you know him."

Getty glanced at Lougheed standing to one side, looking anxious. "If he's the Premier of Alberta, then I'm the King of England," Getty replied.

The guard broke the news to Lougheed that Getty didn't know him. "The Premier's jaw dropped," Getty chuckled. "I don't know why I did it." He rushed over to the scowling Lougheed and promptly rescued him so they could go into the meeting.

Stop Nodding
Don Getty was new to politics when he first won a seat in the Legislature in 1967. As one of the six original Conservatives who formed the Official Opposition, he sat across from Premier Ernest Manning and the Social Credit ministers. Getty had long admired the veteran Premier who was now in his twenty-fifth year as head of the government. "He always sounded so logical." In fact, Getty was so mesmerized by Manning's arguments that he nodded in agreement as the Premier outlined his reasons for certain government actions.

Peter Lougheed, the Leader of the Opposition, noticed the head nodding. Agreeing with the Premier was bad enough, but to demonstrate that agreement was just too much. Lougheed sent Getty a note, "Stop nodding."

WE GET CARDS AND LETTERS

Answering the Mail

Alberta Premiers get bags of mail on every conceivable subject. They take seriously the requests and opinions expressed in the thousands of cards and letters addressed to the Premier's Office each year. Public opinion is the main factor in government decisions. If Premier Manning's ministers couldn't show strong public support for controversial measures, then he instructed them to re-think their plans.

Premier Lougheed's office received about eight hundred letters a month. He had three priorities for dealing with letters. Handwritten ones were number one and often got his personal attention and reply. Lougheed often took a batch home with him to work on in the evening. Typed letters with postage stamps were priority number two and those run through a postage meter were treated with less urgency.

Returning Calls

Premiers also get plenty of phone calls, some they return, others they don't. Eddie Keen, a commentator for CHED Radio in Edmonton, had a Lougheed staff memo fall into his hands. Dated January 7, 1976, it suggested the premier call a determined woman from Thunder Bay, Ontario. For one reason or another, the premier didn't. Keen did and spoke to "a delightful grandmother," visiting her son in Hinton. She identified herself as a Conservative, one who liked Prime Minister Pierre Trudeau.

The woman wanted straight answers from Lougheed about the Tories' plans to run Canada, if they were to form the next federal government. Rumours were flying that the premier would quit Alberta politics to run for the federal Conservative leadership. She wanted to know: what he would do to control big unions, whether statements by miners in Grande Cache that an engineering error had resulted in the loss of millions of tons of coal were true, and how was it possible that in wealthy Alberta a power failure could happen on New Year's Eve, forcing her to celebrate in the dark?

Her final shot was a suggestion Lougheed should forget about the federal leadership. It was all too obvious Alberta needed some looking after. The other Tory leadership candidates didn't escape her sarcasm. "What a lovely bunch of coconuts."

Have a nice day, Mr. Premiers!

ONE FLOOR BELOW

FIRST AND LAST VISIT

Peter Lougheed rose in the gallery to acknowledge the desk pounding of the Alberta MLAs. It was his first visit to the Assembly following his election as leader of the provincial Progressive Conservative Party in 1965. A few seconds later, Neil Crawford, a future Lougheed cabinet minister and government house leader, rose to receive the same greeting. As they settled

The late Grant Notley (left), Leader of the Opposition from 1982 to 1985, and Ray Martin (middle), with Speaker Gerry Amerongen (seated).

into their seats, a page delivered a note: "Mr. Lougheed, welcome to political life. I want to assure you the first twenty-five years are the worst." It was signed by Premier Ernest Manning.

Lougheed suddenly had second thoughts about politics. He said someone was droning on in one of the dullest speeches he had ever heard. "I said to myself do I really want to get into this."

As it turned out, the visit was his last to the Legislature gallery. Crawford, who had been an assistant to Prime Minister John Diefenbaker, knew the value of 'The Chief's' political advice. When the wily federal politician learned about the visit to the Assembly, he sent word to Lougheed to stay away. His advice: wait until you can walk through the door to take your seat as an elected MLA. Two years later, Lougheed did just that.

Social Crediters were carefully watching Lougheed's attempts to revive the provincial Conservatives. Manning was looking for a successor, someone like Lougheed who could take over the leadership. In Manning's view there was little difference between the two parties. Manning admits there were informal discussions to explore the possibility of Lougheed joining Social Credit. Lougheed didn't deny those discussions had taken place. However, he called it a "private matter," preferring that Manning comment. Ray Speaker, a former Socred cabinet minister, filled in some of the details. He said Joe Clark, who was involved in provincial politics at that time, represented Lougheed at meetings in a basement office at the rear of the Legislature. According to Speaker, the future Prime Minister climbed in and out of the basement window so he wouldn't be seen entering the office of one of Manning's aides.

Lougheed and Manning maintained a close association long after the Social Credit Premier left provincial politics. When Lougheed became Premier, they met two or three times a year to discuss current issues. "He was a good counsellor."

BREAKTHROUGH

The Progressive Conservatives won six of ten opposition seats in 1967, making Lougheed Leader of the

Opposition. The Legislature wasn't prepared for so many opposition members, the largest number in twelve years. Journalist Allan Hustak wrote, "The opposition had neither office space nor a research budget. It's business was conducted in the corridors or in the members' lounge. Lougheed, elected in May, would not assume office until the Legislature opened the following February."

Lougheed discovered the traditional distinction between the Legislative Assembly and the Executive Council, the cabinet, had been blurred during the years of large Socred majorities. Bill MacDonald, the Clerk of the Assembly, was also the Clerk of the Executive Council. Just how entwined the Assembly and the government had become was evident when the new Opposition Leader asked what facilities were available. MacDonald said it was up to the Premier and he would arrange "an audience" with him.

Manning did respond to the needs of a larger opposition. Two months after the election he set up a cabinet committee to find space, not only for the opposition but for cabinet members, spread across the city. By the end of the year carpenters were building new offices on the second, third and fourth floors at a cost of almost a million dollars.

TORIES DIG IN

The rejuvenated opposition had a surprise for the Socreds on the opening day of the new session in 1968. Lougheed proposed that an opposition member be named chairman of the Public Accounts Committee, a key position usually held by a government member. When he discussed the proposal with Manning, the Premier was cool, suggesting it would disrupt the opening day. The Tories proposed the change, which was later accepted. "I think that started a lot of things that changed the vitality of the Assembly."

From the opposition side many of the fifty-five government members were almost hidden because they sat on one level, not on three as they are now arranged. Lougheed said one Socred, who hadn't spoken during

the ten weeks of the session, got up to introduce a class of students visiting the Assembly. Don Getty looked over at the member, not realizing his own microphone was open. "Who the hell is that?" he blurted out. The Socred lost his composure and sat down unable to make the introduction.

Lougheed, the rookie, was often guided by the experience of Dr. Hugh Horner, who had been a federal Member of Parliament for ten years before his election to the Legislature. During the 1971 session, Lougheed was ready to oppose a Social Credit bill that would allow the cabinet to establish a new government department with the necessary funds to operate it, before the Legislature had approved its creation. The Opposition Leader was ready to fight the move with "righteous indignation."

Horner whispered, "Don't do that. We'll need it."

Sure enough, the new Conservative cabinet used the Social Credit legislation just four months later. Lougheed said, "We organized the Department of Federal and Intergovernmental Affairs and ran it for eight months."

PROWSE VERSUS MANNING

Politics is largely a contest of personalities. The media creates the impression government and opposition party leaders would barely nod if they met on a back road. That certainly wasn't the case with David Milwyn Duggan, a former mayor of Edmonton, and Conservative leader when the Socreds came to power.

There was no doubt about his opposition to the new reform movement but his actions in the Assembly won the respect of the Socreds. In Manning's view Duggan was one of the best parliamentarians in the Legislature, a wonderful orator. "I had great admiration for him."

That wasn't the case with Captain J. Harper Prowse, who first sat in the Legislature as one of three armed forces members in 1945. When the wartime seats were abolished in 1947, he joined the Liberals and became Mannning's chief opponent. The two men couldn't have been more different. Ernest Watkins had a chance to watch them spar in the Legislature for a few months before Prowse left the ring: "The difference in temperament between them was total; Manning austere, living within his shell, always conscious that this life was only a short prelude to another of greater glory and reward. Prowse a *bon viveur*, enjoying every aspect of life on earth and, never without his memories of the men who had lost their chance of sharing that joy. Prowse sometimes drank too much, Manning did not drink at all."

Captain J. Harper Prowse being sworn in as an Armed Forces Representative (March, 1945).

On one of those occasions, so a version of the story goes, Prowse was back in his place for a night sitting after a dinner break. Early in a stormy debate he tried to get to his feet to blast one of the Socreds. He had so much difficulty getting up he seemed stuck to the chair. Then with one mighty effort, the chair started to rise with him. On the other side, the Socreds were howling. Someone had spread glue on Prowse's chair.

Another version of the incident remembered by former Speaker Arthur Dixon of Calgary makes the Liberals the culprits, spreading the glue not on Prowse's chair but on Hugh John MacDonald's, a Calgary Liberal who later became a supreme court justice. Andy Snaddon, a former correspondent for the Calgary *Herald* in the late '40s, said, "I can remember Prowse thundering across the house in his rich resonant baritone that Manning was the 'Judas' in the Social Credit Movement. On the following Monday, Manning got up and just worked Prowse over right and left."

ARMED FORCES ELECT MEMBERS

The Navy and Air Force representatives walked briskly down the main aisle of the Legislative Assembly accompanied by Premier Ernest Manning and Opposition Leader J. Percy Page. Speaker Peter Dawson introduced two of the three armed forces representatives who had been elected to special wartime seats in the Legislature. Chief Petty Officer Loftus Dudley Ward and Wing Commander Fred C. Colborne, both of Calgary, took their seats on the opposition side with an enthusiatic ovation from the other members. Canadian Army representative, Captain J. Harper Prowse, made his formal entry later. He was still on board a slow ship from Italy, where he was serving with the Loyal Edmonton Regiment. The year was 1945. World War ll was coming to an end. The Legislature created the three special seats to give Alberta servicemen and women a voice in their return to civilian life.

For Fred Colborne the election was his first as a candidate and a voter. "I didn't do any campaigning and I didn't expect to win." The winner of the Distinguished Flying Cross for two probable kills of Nazi U-boats won by one vote. He picked up two more votes on a recount. When the seats were dissolved in 1948, Colborne won re-election as a Socred in Calgary. He became a cabinet minister in 1955 and sat in the Legislature until 1971. Dudley Ward joined the Liberal Party with Harper Prowse but was defeated in the 1948 general election and dropped out of provincial politics. Harper Prowse finally arrived to take his seat and went on to lead the Alberta Liberal Party and the Official Opposition until he resigned in 1958.

During World War l two armed forces representatives were elected to the Legislature in 1917: Nursing Sister Roberta MacAdam and Captain Robert Pierson. The nursing sister was one of two women who won seats, marking the first time women voted in a provincial election and sat in the Legislature.

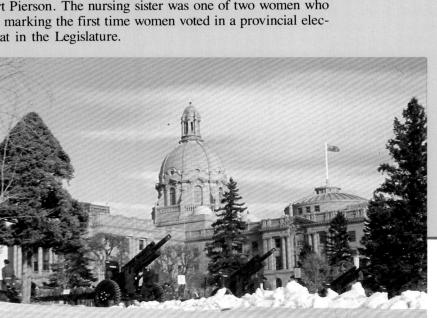

Irene Parlby

Nellie McClung

WOMEN FIGHT FOR POLITICAL EQUALITY

Barriers Fall

Louise McKinney holds a triple honour. Not only was she the first woman to take her seat in the Alberta Legislature, she was the first woman elected to any provincial or federal parliament, and the first elected woman in the British Empire. She ran under the banner of the Non-Partisan League, a farm movement in 1917, but lost at the next election when she switched to the United Farmers of Alberta.

Another winner in the 1917 election was Roberta MacAdam (later Price), a nursing sister elected as one of two overseas representatives in World War I. She gained the distinction of being the first woman to introduce a piece of legislation in the British Empire. It proposed the establishment of the War Veterans Next-of-Kin Association.

Of the twenty-six women who have won seats in the Alberta Legislature, seven have held cabinet posts. Four of the ten women elected in 1986 entered the cabinet of Premier Don Getty. Since 1916 when women first got the vote, there has always been at least one in the legislature.

One of Canada's best known advocates for women's rights was Nellie McClung, a westerner from Ontario. After strenuous campaigning for women's suffrage in Manitoba, she was elected as a Liberal to the Alberta Legislature in 1921 but lost her seat in the next election on the prohibition issue. McClung was a political maverick. She often voted with the UFA government when she agreed with its proposals.

Emily Murphy

Major Victory

McClung was one of five women led by Emily Murphy, the first woman magistrate in the British Empire, who fought the Persons' Case all the way to the Privy Council in England. It ruled women were persons and could be appointed to the Canadian Senate, an important victory in the fight for women's rights in Canada. The other women were: Louise McKinney, Henrietta Edwards and Irene Parlby, a cabinet minister in the UFA government for fourteen years.

Nellie McClung believed strongly that women were morally superior to men and that women should be the main influence in the making of political policies. Her favourite saying, ''Never retract, never explain, never apologize - get the thing done and let them howl.''

Henrietta Muir Edwards

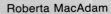

Roberta MacAdam

Louise McKinney

WRONG CHEMISTRY

Looking back at those exchanges in the assembly, Senator Manning admitted he and Prowse were never close. "I found it difficult to have high respect for him. His style didn't appeal to me. It was bombastic. Attack, attack, attack."

Prowse's strategy was the one most opposition leaders employ. He tried to convince the voters his Liberals were a credible alternative to Manning and Social Credit. Although the Liberals doubled their seats in 1952, they still had only four.

Prowse's best chance came as the 1955 election approached. Several controversies had Manning on the defensive. Only one was serious enough to cause the government problems. The province was leasing a building in Edmonton owned by two Socred members, Roy Lee of Taber and John Landeryou of Lethbridge. They were forced to resign their seats.

The crisis grew and showed signs of getting out of hand, so the Premier called an election. The Liberals won fifteen of twenty-two opposition seats but Manning still held a comfortable majority. Prowse quit Alberta politics in 1958. He was appointed to the Senate in 1966.

Incidently, the two Socred members regained their seats, unhurt by the bad publicity. Landeryou, in particular, had a reputation for his ability to turn difficult situations to his own advantage. He decided to confront rumours that he had a drinking problem at one of his campaign meetings. When it was his turn to speak, he began "There are stories going about that I drink a little. That's a lie." He paused to get the full effect. "I want you to know, I drink a lot." The crowd cheered; that was the end of the rumours.

BACK TO NORMAL

Alberta voters returned to the tradition of electing huge government majorities in 1959 and 1963. By the mid-sixties there were only three opposition members; two were Liberals led by Mike Maccagno. Across the aisle were sixty Socreds. "They treated me okay. Manning changed the rules to let the opposition speak twice." Normally, a member speaks once on an issue.

Despite the lopsided representation in the Assembly, Maccagno made his mark. He represented Lac La Biche, a constituency with a large Francophone population. When a resolution dealing with bilingualism came before the Assembly, he decided to make a speech in French. Part way through, one of the government members tipped over backwards in his chair. This happened occasionally to unsuspecting members who leaned back too far. To cover his embarrassment, the red-faced MLA made an unforgiveable comment, "Mr. Speaker, have the member from Lac La Biche talk white." He succeeded only in embarrassing the government and the Social Credit Party at a time when slurs against the French language had become intolerable.

"No one said a word," Maccagno said, obviously too stunned to know what to say. "But I did see Manning giving the member dark looks." In private, the offending MLA probably got far more than a withering look from the Premier for his offensive outburst.

For an opposition leader who didn't want the job, Maccagno's victories were sometimes sweet. During the debate on the government's White Paper on Human Resources, he warned it contained a lot of fine words but action counted more. Then he read glowing statements from what some Socred members thought was the government's white paper. They pounded their desks in approval. Finally Maccagno identified the document as the Constitution of the Soviet Union.

Members on both sides got caught in the friendly crossfire. Dixon remembers an incident when Bill Dickie of Calgary, who was sitting as a Liberal before he joined Lougheed's Conservatives, quoted the Bible to chide the Premier for acting like God in the handling of some situation.

The Premier listened for a few minutes. He had been a student of the Bible for many years and preached on radio every Sunday. Manning simply directed Dickie, a lawyer, to a story in the New Testament, with the exact chapter and verse, in which "a certain lawyer was tempting him."

The architectural detail of the east facade can be seen clearly in the evening light.

SWINGING DOOR

When the Conservatives formed the government in 1971, the Socreds faced life from the opposition benches for the first time in thirty-six years. It was a tough transition, one that took its toll of opposition leaders. Former Premier Harry Strom, Jim Henderson, Bob Clark and Ray Speaker, all former cabinet ministers held the job for varying periods until the 1982 election.

For Ray Speaker, "The toughest part was finding new issues every day. Everyone expects the question period to be entertaining, something new and exciting. I couldn't get up and be a phony. People wanted me to be an actor. I had to feel strongly about an issue."

Speaker's most memorable time in the opposition was in 1982 when three Socreds, New Democrat Grant Notley and Independent Tom Sindlinger staged a 16-hour filibuster - The Battle of the Alamo - that went all night. As a result, the government changed the house rules to set time limits on debate.

After the 1982 election, Speaker Gerard Amerongen recognized the New Democrats as the Official Opposition with Grant Notley as the leader. For Amerongen, it was the second most difficult decision of his fourteen years in the chair. Recognition by the Speaker is important because it confers number two status on the chosen party, a larger budget for research and a cabinet minister's salary for the Opposition Leader.

Both the New Democrats and the Independents [now the Representative Party] had elected two members. Notley argued his party had polled nineteen per cent of the vote compared with four per cent by the Independents; that his party was far more representative of Albertans. The Speaker said politically it would have been far easier to recognize the Independents, because they posed less of a threat to the governing Conservatives.

Gold paint highlights the carved acanthus leaves of the Corinthian capitals.

Amerongen's most difficult decision also involved Notley. During a debate the Opposition Leader raised a point of privilege which involved Premier Lougheed. The Speaker refused to deal with it immediately as called for by the rules. He ruled it would be unfair to hear the charge because the Premier was out of the province. Notley would have to wait until Lougheed returned in a few days. The Opposition Leader appealed the ruling to the house, but it was defeated by the large Conservative majority. The Speaker was greatly upset by the appeal and comments that resulted from his ruling. "I was shocked by the member's attitude in appealing my ruling."

DIFFERENCES FORGOTTEN

The intense feelings generated in the Assembly rarely carried over into their personal dealings with each other. Members of all political parties blend into a large family, quick to launch stinging attacks when the issues are important but just as quick to forgive and forget. This closing of ranks was never more apparent than in October 1984 when Grant Notley was killed in a plane crash on a flight to his constituency. Larry Shaben, a Conservative cabinet minister, was aboard the flight but survived the crash.

The job of Opposition Leader fell to Ray Martin, who had been a Member for only two years. "I couldn't be Grant. I'd never be the parliamentarian he was. I learned you have to be thick skinned and have a sense of humour or you'll go mad. Politics is an extremely stressful occupation. If you can't stand conflict, don't get into political life."

Martin's most frustrating day in opposition came during a question period early in his career. He was trying to question Premier Lougheed but ran afoul of Speaker Amerongen who stopped him several times for violations of the rules.

"This place is a joke," Martin said, slamming down his papers. He stomped out of the Assembly, not by the side doors the members ordinarily used, but right down the main aisle to the front doors. The members sat silently wondering what Martin would do if the doors were locked. They weren't and he disappeared, the door banging behind him.

Martin viewed question period from the opposition side as "show and tell, theatre. Anything to get people interested." He's convinced people are confused about the role of the opposition, and that all politicians are not held in high regard with the result democracy is suffering.

TRAGIC MOMENTS REMEMBERED

Members Killed

In times of personal tragedy the MLAs put aside their political differences. Premier Peter Lougheed underlined that fact in 1984 when he repeated an observation made by Opposition Leader Jim Henderson on an earlier occasion. "In moments such as this, there are no two sides of the House."

On at least four occasions they have met to pay tribute to fellow Members who met sudden death. Three Alberta cabinet ministers and a leader of the opposition have died in accidents, others have survived near misses.

In 1953 the Social Credit Minister of Agriculture, David Ure of Red Deer, died in a head-on collision with a truck forty miles west of Edmonton.

In 1965 Norman Willmore of Edson, the Social Credit Minister of Lands and Forests was killed in a head-on collision with a truck seventy miles west of Edmonton.

In 1973, the Conservative Minister of Telephones and Utilities, Len Werry of Calgary, was killed when his car slid on an icy curve 120 miles west of Edmonton and struck the rear wheels of a tractor-trailer truck.

In 1984, Opposition Leader Grant Notley of Spirit River-Fairview, narrowly escaped serious injury when his car hit an elk in the Peace River area. One month later, he was one of six people killed when their plane crashed on a hillside near High Prairie. Conservative cabinet minister Larry Shaben was on the same plane but survived the crash.

In 1985, another cabinet minister, Neil Webber, and Harry Alger, the MLA for Highwood, escaped without serious injury when their plane caught fire during takeoff from Calgary.

RECORD HOLDERS

Gordon Taylor, the former member for Drumheller and a cabinet minister, holds the record as the longest sitting member in the Alberta Legislature - 39 years. He sat both as a Socred and an Independent. Taylor was first elected in 1940 and served until 1979. He resigned to run as a Progressive Conservative for a seat in the House of Commons, which he won.

Gordon Kesler, a rodeo performer from southern Alberta, holds the record for the shortest career in the Assembly. The leader of the Western Canada Concept and the member for Olds-Didsbury, sat as a member of the opposition for only one session in 1982. He was defeated in the '82 election and quit politics.

Peter Lougheed holds a different record. Until he became Leader of the Opposition, the job had turned into a graveyard for political ambition. Not one politician who held the job before him had become Premier. On two previous occasions when Albertans wanted to change government parties, they put their trust in new movements. The United Farmers of Alberta swept the Liberals out of office; Social Credit, in turn, destroyed the farmers' party. Lougheed's Conservatives broke the historic jinx after just four years in opposition.

C.W. Cross, a member of the first Alberta cabinet, was the only MLA to represent two constituencies. In the 1913 General Election he ran as a Liberal candidate in Edmonton and Edson. Cross won both seats and represented them in the assembly.

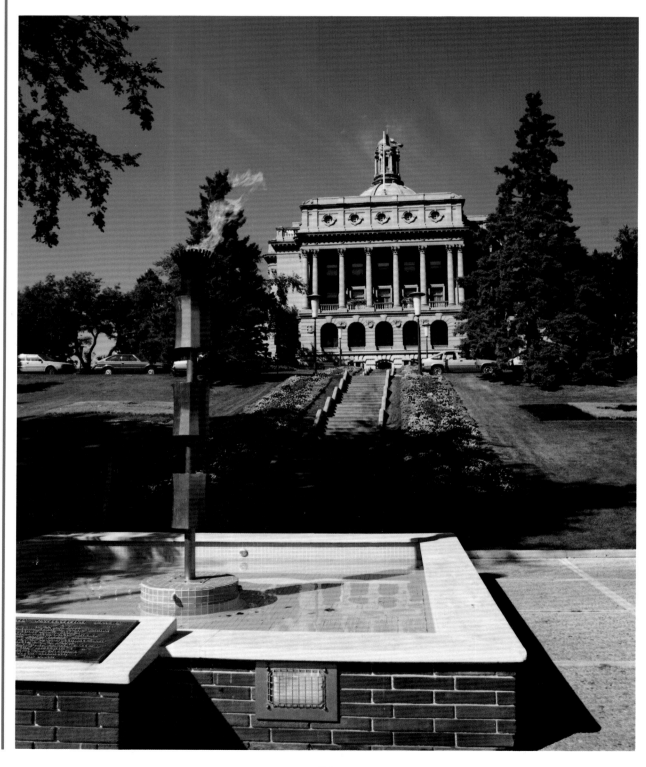

THE VIEW FROM THE PRESS GALLERY

The Press Gallery is located above the speaker's chair at the east end of the Assemby.

WHOOPS!

O ne of the first sights the members must have seen when they first settled into the new Assembly were reporters' faces peering over the edge of the press gallery. The eyes peering down from above have kept watch ever since, witnessing a major part of the province's political history unfold.

Up one storey from the floor and behind the Speaker, reporters sit at a counter, running the width of the chamber. Two pillars cut off the view of much of the chamber below for those unlucky enough to get stuck behind them. The gallery is so narrow anyone tilting back in a chair blocks traffic in and out. Plug-ins are additions of the electronic age so that reporters can tape the proceedings. A ledge on the writing counter is designed to prevent falling equipment from endangering those below.

Accidents do happen. A reporter from Canadian Press rushed to his seat in the gallery just as the Speaker began the prayer to start the day's sitting. He threw his notebook on the counter and bowed his head. The notebook took one bounce and flew over the edge, landing near Clerk Assistant Warren Graves. Horrified by his own clumsiness, the reporter scribbled an apology.

When a page returned the notebook an attached note said, "One notebook doth not a prorogation make!" A reference to the long tradition of reporters showering the members with paper at the end of a session. The flying notebook wasn't the first or the last missile attack, which led gallery veterans to conclude the appearance of carpenters soon after to build a canopy over the Speaker's exposed chair was at least an indirect result of the flying notebook and a sensible decision.

THE REFUGE

Directly behind the gallery was the press work area, another long, narrow room where reporters often worked far into the night producing the copy for tomorrow's headlines. Typical of most newsrooms, it was piled high with paper and lacked any real privacy for reporters trying to dig up exclusive stories, but it was home.

After seventy-five years the number of gallery members had long outgrown the space. Television and radio reporters moved to the Legislature's basement and another location on the fifth floor in the '70s. Print reporters stayed put until the major renovation of the assembly in 1987 moved them to new offices on the first floor. The venerable old work room now houses a TV control room and a radio studio for broadcasts of the assembly proceedings, plus equipment for the sound system.

Unfortunately much of the gallery's history from those early days has died with the people who made it. Reporters who so meticulously recorded the politicians' antics didn't keep an account of their own activities. However, newspaper accounts give a brief glimpse of life in the gallery. The Edmonton *Journal* ran a story at the conclusion of the 1913 session showing how at least one tradition has survived. Once the formalities ended, reporters responded just the way they have at the conclusion of every session since then - throwing the members' words back at them.

"The Lieutenant-Governor and his suite retire. The House breaks up and the legislators, like school boys released from arduous tasks, respond to the pelting of papers they get from the members of the press gallery."

A HARD HAT AREA FOR MLAS

The Paper Blizzard

The traditional paper toss over the side of the press gallery at the conclusion of a legislative session has its moments of danger. Just ask Bob Bogle, a former Conservative cabinet minister. His desk was in the direct path of torn-up copies of Hansard, the daily record of the proceedings, and other potential missiles, like bills, thick reports, anything introduced into the Assembly.

On one occasion in the rush to prepare the wastebaskets of paper to throw the members' words back, someone didn't tear-up all the material. The heavy booklets plummeted the twenty feet or more to the floor with a thud, narrowly missing Bogle. Years before in a similar incident, a coke bottle almost hit a Social Credit member.

The tradition drew frowns at one prorogation when reporters hurled the paper before the Speaker left the chamber. The indiscretion produced a sharp note from the Parliamentary Counsel, the legal interpreter of all things parliamentary, outlining the proper etiquette to be followed in future.

Editorial Comment

More creative reporters have used the paper throw to draw attention to controversial issues which dominated debate and even to comment on the members' performance. When the Lougheed government bought Pacific Western Airlines in 1974, reporters sailed paper planes across the Assembly. One session was so boring only a single piece of paper fluttered down.

Mark Byington, a former legislature reporter for CFRN in Edmonton, said one of the biggest coups pulled by the gallery was the use of the shredder in Premier Lougheed's office to prepare the paper. Obviously an inside job because reporters rarely got past Lougheed's receptionist.

A Mini-Shower

A paper shower of another kind preceded the big throw as reporters and members restlessly endured the final days of most sessions. The exchange of notes between the press gallery and the members reflected a certain giddiness. Byington listened to a Social Credit member administer a blistering attack on Merv Leitch, a Conservative cabinet minister. Byington sent a note to Leitch: "How much are you asking for an assassination? We have $37.50." The reply came back: "The cabinet can leave you with a balance of $37.00."

Members of the press gallery.

"ANOTHER ROUND PLEASE"

Two Quart Speech

Before a sound system was installed in the Assembly members almost had to shout to overcome the poor acoustics and the normal noise level. *Herald* reporter Fred Kennedy remembered speakers like William Fallow, a Socred cabinet minister, who kept the pages busy refilling his water glass to soothe his parched throat.

Kennedy wrote in his memoirs that he and Tom Mansell of the Edmonton *Journal* decided to have some fun during one of Fallow's forty minute speeches. They diverted a page's attention as he prepared to deliver another glass of water to the thirsty minister. Instead of water, the page re-entered the Assembly with a full glass of gin and paused behind a government member "who was known for his penchant to walk on occasion with John Barleycorn. He was sitting in his chair half asleep when the odour of the glass of gin wafted in his direction. He straightened up as if he had been shot, looked behind him, saw the glass on the tray, sniffed once more and then reached for the glass with a murmur of apology to the startled page boy."

Kennedy said the member suddenly came to life and applauded every government speech with great enthusiasm. When he applauded the Conservative leader's speech with the same enthusiasm, Premier Aberhart "turned in his chair, glanced at him, frowned, and a fellow member finally led him out of the chamber."

LUCKY BREAK

Another of those glimpses comes from Fred Kennedy, a reporter for the Calgary *Herald* and later the *Albertan*, who covered Alberta for well over half a century. He got his first taste of political reporting when he visited the Legislature on his way back to Calgary from a double hanging at the Fort Saskatchewan Jail in 1923.

Kennedy moved into the gallery seven years later and fell into the kind of scoop every reporter dreams about.

After his first week he was still trying to sort out where to go and who to see. One morning, before anyone else arrived, he was sitting in the gallery, feeling sorry for himself and fiddling with the telegraph key used to send stories to his newsroom. "... I heard

Left to right: Press Gallery members Joe Taylor, Russ Shepherd, Desmond Bill, and Harry Carrigan, with MLA Jonn Hillman, seated.

the door to the work room of the press gallery open. A moment later, someone shoved two long sheets of paper over my right shoulder. By the time I had grasped them, the figure of a girl was just disappearing behind the closing door.''

Kennedy thought it was a routine press release. What he had received without any effort was the draft of the official constitutional amendment that was to return control of resource development to the province from the federal government - the source of most of Alberta's wealth after Leduc Number One blew in 1947. ''My reputation as a hot-shot reporter was now assured.''

Gallery members of that day were a lot closer to the members than they are today. Even hot-shots like Fred Kennedy found nothing objectionable about supplementing their incomes by writing speeches for any member willing to pay a $5 fee. The practice ended when Social Credit came to power.

Today's reporters would consider speech writing a serious conflict of interest. Most are reluctant even to tell politicians or their assistants how to get media coverage. Chris Dean of CFRN in Edmonton said, ''We'll tell them about deadlines, like don't call a news conference at five-fifteen and expect to get it on the Six O'Clock News. But we won't give advice.''

GALLERY HEYDAY

Reporters vied for seats in the gallery to watch the world's first Social Credit experiment in 1935. Membership rose to over a hundred as the major newspapers from across North America and overseas sent their own reporters. The most fascinating imports were Gregori and Sonya Demkatov from the Soviet National News Agency in Moscow. Their suite in the Macdonald Hotel became a favourite gathering place for reporters. The two Soviets disappeared as mysteriously as they arrived. They checked out one day without saying goodbye and that was the last anyone saw of them.

The Moscow connection didn't end there. Another news agency wanted details of the ''social revolution,'' underway in Alberta. As secretary of the Press Gallery Association, Kennedy got the request and cabled a story. Shortly after, he filed a second and final story. Eventually a bank draft for $45 dollars arrived. Four years later with Canada at war, two RCMP officers appeared at his desk requesting information about his work for the Soviet government. After a frantic search, Kennedy pulled copies of his two stories from a desk drawer. They took the file and promised to be in touch. He never heard from them again.

THE HOT WAR

The Aberhart era was a reporter's delight. Alberta was a maelstrom of conflicting forces as Social Credit tried to change the monetary system to end economic depressions for all time. Check these confrontations for headline potential:

- The provincial and federal governments and the courts duelling constantly over who could do what.
- The bankers under seige and fighting back.
- The Aberhart loyalists and the insurgents demanding quick implementation of Social Credit theories.
- Four stormy sessions of the Legislature in 1937.
- A Social Credit member and Major Douglas's representative jailed for libel and counselling to murder as a result of the ''Bankers' Toadies,'' pamphlet.
- Lieutenant-Governor John Bowen refused to give Royal Assent to three bills.

Add the constant attacks by Alberta's major newspaper. Is it any wonder Aberhart and his cabinet ministers retaliated whenever they could? Kennedy reported another attack on September 19, 1937 by Aberhart on the newspapers in a radio broadcast from Edmonton. ''Some of these creatures with mental hydrophobia will be taken in hand and their biting and barking will cease.''

After a particularly vicious editorial attack, William Fallow, a Social Credit cabinet minister glared up at the press gallery: ''Mr. Speaker, if I were the representative of the Edmonton *Journal*, I would apologize to the honourable members of this house, get down on my hands and knees, crawl outside and pause on the way to apologize to the janitor.''

Flower beds brighten the south grounds of the Legislature.

PRESS GAG FAILS

The rhetoric was mild compared with The Accurate News and Information Act introduced by Aberhart in the fall of 1937, designed to curb criticism of the government. Newspapers across Canada and Europe condemned the bill. One overseas paper likened Aberhart to "a little Hitler." The Edmonton *Journal* won a Pulitzer Award for leading a successful attack on the legislation.

The Socreds struck again in March, 1938. The Legislature convicted Don Brown, a Journal writer, on a charge of breaching the privileges of the House. At issue were two paragraphs in the Journal column, "Under the Dome," which the Social Credit member for Medicine Hat, Dr. J.L. Robinson, claimed misrepresented him. The Speaker was instructed to issue a warrant for Brown's arrest and detention in the Lethbridge Jail. The whole thing turned into a comic opera when the assembly accepted a Liberal motion to release Brown, who hadn't been arrested.

Edmonton *Journal* Pulitzer Prize winning reporters, Jim P. Rennie, Joe Dwyer, and Don Brown, authors of the "Under the Dome" column in the 1930s.

Mike Maccagno, Leader of the Opposition, with members of the Press Gallery (1960).

EXCITEMENT GONE

When Andy Snaddon moved into the Calgary *Herald's* spot in the gallery in 1948, the explosive issues of the '30s had faded. "The Social Crediters weren't the liveliest crew. Covering one of their conventions was like attending a church social. The exciting highlight was always when the Macdonald Hotel brought in the Baked Alaska desert with sparklers trailing." Alf Hooke's recitations and a church choir completed the entertainment. The party shook that image briefly in the early '80s when someone decided to liven up a convention luncheon in Calgary with a belly dancer. Reporters speculated correctly, as history demonstrated, it would take more than the gyrations of a dancer to revive Social Credit.

For Snaddon and the other reporters, working in the gallery was a daily trip into a time warp. Other than new faces peering over the edge to catch the action, the physical environment had changed little in decades. Each typewriter still had a telegraph key beside it. On big stories, like the provincial budget, operators sat beside the reporters and sent the copy as it poured hot from the typewriter. It was a scene from a Grade B movie.

Good stories were harder to find than in the Aberhart days. "We'd cut each other's throats to get a story." Despite the competition, reporters got along well with each other and with the members. Opposition Leader Mike Maccagno was famous for his spaghetti dinners and card games for gallery members. The Socreds made sure reporters got invitations to all the Assembly's social functions.

Snaddon, who later became an editor and publisher, noted a difference in today's reporters. "They're more like hunters. Sometimes, you can almost sense the instinct for a kill when you watch them interviewing some politicians. They're out to get him, What they're reaching for is a good story. That's legitimate enough."

He had some of that killer instinct, too. When his daughter became a radio reporter, she interviewed a Socred politician. He told her, "You're just as much a bastard as your old man was." Snaddon accepted the comment as a compliment.

During the '50s events begin to heat up again. Dick Snell, Snaddon's successor, won a National Newspaper Award for his stories on dealings between Socred members and the province's Treasury Branches, which helped to precipitate the 1955 election.

Crowded television camera platforms were an eyesore, as well as a hazard.

THE ELECTRONIC AGE

With the arrival of radio and television reporters, members suddenly became more image conscious. Rambling speeches might get by in the Assembly, but politicians had to master the short clip to be a face on the evening news. New Democratic Party Leader Grant Notley was always ready with punchy bursts reporters loved.

No one handled television quite as well as Peter Lougheed. He was acknowledged as the smoothest, most relaxed politician in front of the camera. Early in his political career, the future Premier worked on his technique with a friend, Gordon Love of CFCN in Calgary. He taught Lougheed the basics every night at eleven-thirty for a week in the station's studio.

Gone were the folksy news conferences in Premier Manning's office followed by a trip to the basement TV studio for interviews. The ever-growing number of reporters and camera crews moved across the hall from the Premier's office to the cabinet room, often for "availability sessions." The government jargon meant the Premier didn't have any announcements, but he was available to answer questions. He resisted all efforts by the gallery to schedule regular news conferences. Lougheed said he was afraid reporters would expect him to answer questions that his ministers should be answering.

Lougheed rarely got caught in "scrums," hallway interviews from which reporters hope the right question will produce a nugget advancing the story of the day. Lougheed usually arrived early at his office far ahead of the reporters, then emerged only rarely. When he did

arrive later, the veteran jogger often tossed off a one-liner and was home-free in his office before the cameras could fire up.

When the house was in session, he often stopped to give more detail on matters raised in question period. Reporters had to be fast as he breezed by or took a more circuitous route to his office. At times the exercise turned into a flying circus when the Premier moved at a brisk pace with cameras, microphones, lights and reporters all in full flight to catch something usable for the supper hour news or tomorrow's paper.

STAIRWAY JOURNALISM

Sheila Pratt, a columnist for the Calgary *Herald*, felt the brunt of Lougheed's scorn when she attempted to question him about a police investigation into the actions of a senior civil servant. She pursued the Premier down a back stairway, asking, "Do you know about the investigation and what are you going to do about it?"

Lougheed brushed past her with the curt reply, "I hope you sleep well tonight."

Despite media complaints of Tory attempts to manage the news and some talk about the need for a stronger opposition, Lougheed won more seats each time he went to the polls. He didn't quite match the unofficial Tory slogan, "Seventy-nine seats in '79," but he did win seventy-four. As a result, Patrick O'Callaghan, the publisher of the Edmonton *Journal* proclaimed his newspaper the unofficial opposition and increased the Journal's Legislature bureau to about nine reporters.

The move by O'Callaghan didn't bother Lougheed as long as the reporting remained factual. He gave that message directly to the *Journal* publisher. Lougheed said it's natural for the media to support the underdog and he would too. At the time, many reporters didn't want to be seen as the opposition, out to get the government. Chris Dean said, ''Some reporters may be trying to get the government, most are simply trying to get information and do a job.''

An old rule says that when people of opposing political parties complain that coverage is biased, chances are it's balanced. During one session, some Conservative members complained to Dean, that the media were supporting the opposition. Liberal and Representative Party members accused reporters of being pro-government.

Premier Don Getty introduced a different style in dealing with reporters. He started his first term ready to comment on practically everything. When controversies developed, Pratt and Dean said the Premier blamed the media and changed the rules.

Topics must be submitted ahead of time; no questions from left field. The Premier said he finds more cynicism about government in the media and some are still acting like the official opposition.

period. Because of the placement of the cameras on the side of the Assembly behind the opposition desks, viewers rarely saw any more than the backs of their heads. When Opposition Leader Bob Clark retired in 1981, the press gallery gave him a hockey sweater with ''Clark'' and ''Leader of the Opposition'' on the back, just in case he might make a political come-back.

A major escape valve for frustrations is the annual press gallery Christmas party for the members and civil servants in the building. The reporters poke fun at the politicians and the issues using skits and their own versions of Christmas songs. Remember the government's controversial choice of Mount Allan for downhill skiing in the '88 Olympics, despite its unpredictable snow cover? The gallery serenaded government members with, ''On Top of Mount Allan, Let it snow, let it snow;'' What better Christmas greeting than, ''We wish you a higher oil price, We wish you a higher oil price ...''

Asbestos workers and insulators demonstrate at the Legislature grounds.

LEARNING TO LAUGH

The politicians and the reporters in the gallery have always had a love-hate relationship. Like all relationships forged by necessity, their dealings are always cautious, sometimes prickly, even explosive. Only a sense of humour makes life together tolerable. A few examples:

Television made familiar faces out of Conservative cabinet ministers, but it didn't do much for opposition members as they battled the government in question

When the action dragged in the Assembly, gallery members started voting each day on the tackiest tie worn by a cabinet minister. The result was the ''Julian Koziak Rotten Tie Award,'' given out on the final day of the session. The Conservative cabinet minister was often the butt of jokes for his choice of ties and other apparel. Because the voting had been hit and miss at best, the first award went to Premier Lougheed. He proudly wore the fourteen foot tie at his desk in the Assembly.

You won't find reporters and politicians admitting it too often, but the truth is - they need each other.

BREAKING THE BUDGET

Dynamic Duo

Andy Snaddon of the Calgary *Herald* and Bill Drever of the Edmonton *Journal* had a standing bet in the late '40s to see who could find out within an hour what the Socreds had decided in their latest caucus meeting. Snaddon had an advantage living at the Corona Hotel on Jasper Avenue, a few blocks from the Legislature. He had easy access to the Social Credit members from outside Edmonton, who stayed there during sittings of the Assembly.

However, the members tended to be tight-lipped because they disliked the Calgary and Edmonton newspapers for their attacks on the Socreds. Snaddon and Drever devised a way around this problem. They looked for disgruntled backbenchers who hadn't made it into the cabinet or received any of the other political rewards. With a little persistence, the two reporters usually extracted enough information to put a story together.

Who Told?

Their biggest triumph came just before Premier Ernest Manning, who was also the Provincial Treasurer, was about to present the government's annual budget. Snaddon and Drever got the main details and fired them off to their papers the day before Manning made his budget address. When he revealed the proposed government spending for the next year, Snaddon and Drever listened smugly, knowing there was nothing of importance that wasn't already spread across the front pages of their newspapers.

In the British parliamentary tradition such a leak would result in the resignation of the minister involved. But Premier Manning wasn't about to resign. He certainly hadn't leaked the budget. Only three other people, including the Premier, knew its contents, so the usual caucus back benchers weren't any help in this case. Snaddon still isn't saying who talked and why.

Manning was furious but there was nothing he could do. On another occasion the Premier was so upset by the two for breaking stories on government decisions, that he instructed the caucus to stay away from them. Two of the freer spirits among the Socreds, Roy Lee of Taber and John Landeryou of Lethbridge, weren't going to be told who they could talk to, even by the Premier. They parked their car in front of the Legislature and signalled to Snaddon and Drever to come back to the Corona for lunch with them.

''Who came along but Manning. Landeryou tooted his horn and waved at him so he couldn't fail to see who was in the car with him.''

The Alberta coat of arms is carved on the door to the Assembly.

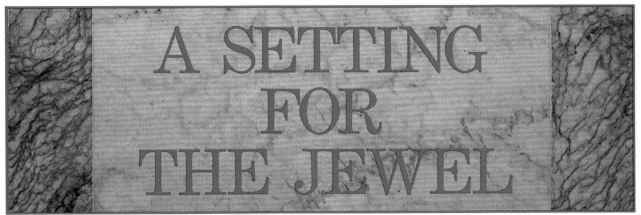

A SETTING FOR THE JEWEL

GREEN SCHEME WINS

By the 1970s conditions were right to complete the Legislature grounds facing north to Edmonton's downtown business area. World energy prices were soaring and Premier Peter Lougheed's Progressive Conservative government had raised provincial royalties to give Albertans a bigger share of the wealth from their own resources.

For decades the view from the Legislature's front doors was a narrow strip of grass with a row of evergreens. Beyond that, a steep bank leading to 97th Avenue, where traffic roared in and out of the river valley. More government buildings, old houses and ugly parking lots completed the dowdy view. Contrast this with the south view, a mass of trees, shrubs and flowers overlooking the river valley and the site of Fort Edmonton. Something had to be done to the north grounds.

As early as 1928 the United Farmers of Alberta government bought the two blocks on the east side of 109th Street to build the first of a series of government buildings. A long range beautification plan included the area from 107th to 109th Street, and south to the Legislature. Another suggestion was to develop terraced gardens on the west side of 109th Street, but it was turned into a parking lot.

Depression, World War ll and the oil boom pre-occupied the Aberhart and Manning governments. However, they never lost sight of the day when the setting would be complete. Successive Public Works ministers bought properties as they came up for sale within the proposed development area. Demand for government office space led to the construction of the Natural Resources Building, the Administration Building and the Agriculture Building. The federal government built the Federal Building on the corner of 107 Street and 99 Avenue.

The steady traffic flow on 97 Avenue disappeared, threaded through an underpass two blocks long. The sprawling Transportation Building on the east side of the grounds has fallen to the wrecker's ball. The Terrace Building on the river side is scheduled for future demolition, removing the last obstacle to an uncluttered view.

Below ground are two cavernous parking garages, and a pedway system, with space for art and other exhibits. It connects the Legislature with the Legislature Annex, originally the Agriculture Building, the Haultain Building, formerly the Administration Building, and the Bowker Building, formerly the Natural Resources Building. The pedway will connect with the Grandin Light Rail Transit station and the Federal Building. Strollers below ground can catch a glimpse of activity above ground through a fascinating triple-mirror periscope.

Left: The Legislature and grounds from the southwest.
Right: This mirror is part of the periscope system that links the pedway with the grounds above. The Legislature Annex is in the background.
Below: Albertans use the Legislature grounds for a variety of occasions.
Below right: Flower beds border the south staircase.

A PLACE TO ENJOY

By 1974 the Conservative government had the determination and the money to start work. First, it held an architectural competition to select an architect and a design for the proposed Alberta Centre, on fifty-seven acres of prime real estate. John 'Scotty' McIntosh of the Edmonton architectural firm of McIntosh, Workun & Chernenko was named project architect. The firm's Green Scheme — get rid of cars, stop construction of new office buildings, make it a place to enjoy — won over three dozen other proposals.

Barricades went up in 1979, earth movers gouged huge mounds of dirt, and concrete spans moved into place. The final cost, $62,000,000. Inflation and overruns had pushed it $19,000,000 over the original estimate. When the barricades came down, the parking lots and old houses had disappeared. The area was transformed into a park with fountains, pools and walkways, leading up to the Legislature's stately facade.

A huge reflecting pool added another dimension to the view. Reporters quickly named it "Lake Lougheed." Young people had a new wading pool on hot summer days. The open space also provided plenty of room for demonstrators to march on the Legislature and voice their demands.

RAVE NOTICES

Development of the south grounds began in 1912 and developed slowly with the planting of Russian poplar, American mountain ash, elm, birch and evergreens. Plaques and memorials throughout the grounds mark historic events, like the province's Golden Jubilee in 1955. Newspaper stories in the 1920s reported how the spacious lawns and colourful flower beds were attracting many visitors. The headlines proclaimed, ''Alberta's Seat of Government Great Credit,'' and ''Beauty Reigns Supreme … ''

Floodlights on the dome added some glitz to the troubled times of the '30s. A temporary welcome arch rose at the 109th Street entrance to mark the Royal Visit to Alberta in 1939. A new bandstand replaced the old one in 1950, the same year the driveways were paved.

The floral arrangements grew in beauty and complexity each year. By 1961 a new government greenhouse was supplying a hundred and fifty thousand plants every summer to the grounds and thirty provincial government properties around the city. Many future doctors, dentists and lawyers from the University of Alberta found summer jobs at the greenhouse assisting the permanent staff of eighty gardeners.

THE DISAPPEARING TREE

Where Oh Where?

Several recreational facilities eventually covered the Fort Edmonton site. The east bowling green was built in 1923, the west green in 1932, a bandshell in 1959, and a skating rink was added in 1986. Newly planted trees brought beauty and shade to what some newspaper stories referred to as ''the desert.''

One morning, gardeners checking the area noticed one of their trees had suddenly disappeared, literally dropped out of sight. As they peered at the spot where only the day before the tree had stood, they saw a hole at least twenty feet deep. But what had been holding the dirt and tree in place?

The hole was an abandoned well. At some point in the Fort's history workmen placed planks over it, as a safety precaution to prevent anyone from falling down the hole, then piled dirt on top, enough to support a small tree. Eventually the wood rotted and gravity did the rest. The tree fell into the hole. Fortunately it was discovered before some unsuspecting person, strolling on the grounds, followed the tree into the well. A permanent cover closed the hole and the case of the disappearing tree was solved and forgotten.

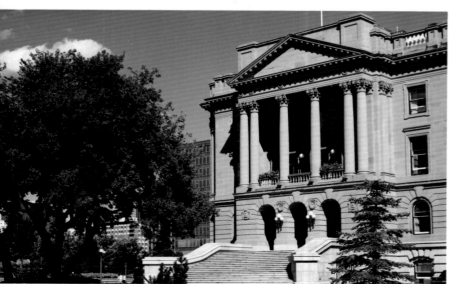

This page, above left: An Indian tipi on the south lawn of the Legislature.
Above: The Legislature provides a stately backdrop for summer activities.
Left: The Legislature is a place that all Albertans can enjoy.
Next page, top: The Canadian flag flies over the Legislative Assembly.
Bottom: The flag of Alberta graces the east and west entrances.

90

FLAGS OVER THE LEGISLATURE

Which Flag?

When Canada's new red and white Maple Leaf flag became official in 1965, it presented a problem for the Alberta Government. Certainly, it would be flown over the Legislature, but there must be a place for the Union Jack, which was still the Lieutenant-Governor's flag, as the Queen's representative.

Fred Colborne, the Minister of Public Works, proposed that the Union Jack fly over the front entrance to the Legislature, where the Lieutenant-Governor's office is situated. The new Canadian flag would then fly over the Legislative Assembly to indicate the Canadian character of that institution.

Later in the 1960s, Alberta adopted its own blue provincial flag with the Alberta crest, without the long and rancorous debate that surrounded the Canadian flag. Now, the Lieutenant-Governor's standard, a new flag, flies over the main entrance, two provincial flags over the east and west entrances, and the Canadian flag over the Assembly.

Above: The original design for the Legislature grounds (1910).
Top centre: 97th Avenue and 109th Street, northwest of the Legislature grounds during reconstruction of the grounds.

Above: A U.S. Air Force C-54 Skymaster transport plane flies over the Legislature (1942).
Bottom left: An aerial view of the Legislature, showing the grounds under construction.
Below: The Legislature and surrounding area; an aerial view from the southeast.

The government greenhouse supplies plants for the
floral displays at the Legislature grounds.

The shape of the fountain to the north of the building
echoes the shape of the dome.

Flower boxes and benches compliment the new north Legislature grounds.

Pools beautify the Legislature grounds and provide an ideal playground during hot Alberta summers.

NEW ATTRACTIONS

Alberta celebrated Canada's Centennial with major new projects to add even more beauty and vitality to the Legislature grounds. Edmontonians walking and driving on Christmas Eve in 1966 received an unexpected gift. The Legislature suddenly burst on to the night skyline. Newly installed floodlights showed off the building for miles around. A week later on New Year's Eve, Premier Manning inaugurated the Centennial Year by lighting an Eternal Flame, fed by natural gas atop a stainless steel standard set in an ornamental pool.

Twenty years later, a new lighting project made the grounds and the rotunda sparkle even more during the Christmas Season. With the touch of a red button Premier Don Getty threw a master switch to turn on eighty thousand lights. The opening of a new skating rink turned the grounds into a year-round recreation area.

In the summer of 1967, another reminder of the Centennial took root on the grounds. The Alberta crest bloomed through the care and ingenuity of government gardeners. They planted seven thousand carpet bedding plants. When they ran short of blue sky for the display, the gardeners dyed santolinas, small foliage plants, to resemble the sky in the crest.

Another gift for Canada's birthday, the Centennial Carillon, rang out across the river valley from high in the Legislature's dome in December 1966. Douglas Millson, the organist and choirmaster at Robertson-Wesley United Church, was Alberta's first provincial carilloneur. Seated alone at a keyboard in the Carillon Room on the Legislature's fifth floor, he played regular concerts for thirteen years. Two other carilloneurs, Bob DeFreece and Mark Sirett continue to perform everything from classical to pop.

The ornate room with a ceiling of stained glass and symbolic paintings is the ideal setting to play this musical instrument from Renaissance times. Carillons of that era had as many as fifty-two bells. The Legislature's carillon gets its sounds from metal rods, which measure up to twenty-eight inches in length. When struck, they produce a tinkling tone, which is broadcast through the speakers in the cupola on the dome. The rods can produce the sounds of 391 bells. The carillon cost $60,000; today, it's valued from a quarter to half a million dollars. Most people living around the Legislature enjoy the music. However, it does produce the odd complaint from nearby apartment dwellers trying to sleep on weekends.

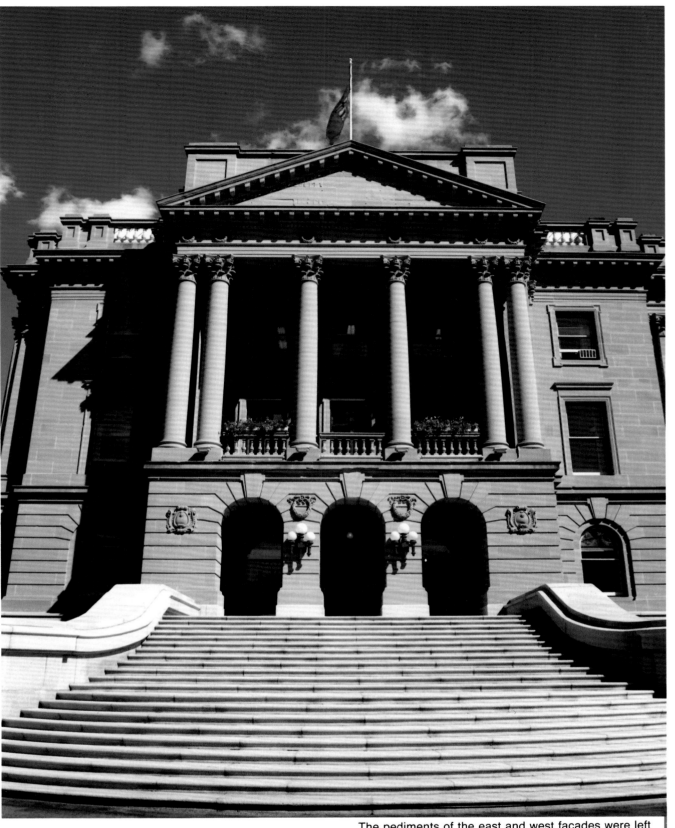

The pediments of the east and west facades were left unfinished. These triangular areas are usually decorated with relief sculpture.

STARTING FROM SCRATCH

When the Canadian Parliament created Alberta and Saskatchewan from the Northwest Territories in 1905, Regina simply switched from a territorial to a provincial capital. It made sense for the existing library to change the name on its door and carry on business as usual. Alberta received $6,113.25 to set up shop in Edmonton or wherever the new capital would be. Not a lot to launch a library, even in the century's early years.

The library's first location was on the second floor of the old Empire Block at 101 Street and Jasper Avenue, the first home of the provincial government. Fortunately, it had a good friend in Premier Alexander Rutherford. When the plans were drawn for the new Legislature he made sure that one of his favourite projects got a central location in the new Legislature, directly behind the main marble staircase.

Even with his influential support, there was no lavish spending in the early days. The library bought its first books and materials with an expenditure of $170.25 for the last four months of 1905 and Alberta's first four months as a province. The appropriation for 1906 was $750. Total spending for the library today is about a million dollars a year. For years the library had a dual role, serving the Legislature as well as communities across the province by sending boxes of books to those places where no other service was available.

Alberta weekly newspapers have long been an important part of the library's collection. Librarian Edith Gostick got a start one morning in 1948 when she was opening a batch of newly arrived newspapers. One of them had a strange odour. She explained in a letter to the editor of the Amisk Advocate: ''The paper arrived this morning and attached to it was some putrid meat which I later discovered was mink, which evidently was in the same mail bag as your newspaper. The paper was spoiled and the smell was terrible. We threw the whole thing out.''

The latest addition to the library is a video tape service. It provides news clips and public affairs items involving members of the Legislature shown on the Edmonton TV stations as well as supplying a video record of the daily question period.

The Legislature Library preserves a sense of the province's exciting history. It has welcomed members of the Royal Family and thousands of other visitors to its gracious surroundings. Until the 1960s two cannons from old Fort Edmonton guarded the library balcony. Members of the armed forces came regularly to polish them during the Second World War. The cannons now are kept at the Provincial Museum for use in displays. The province's first Mace has moved from its display case in the library to a new spot near the Speaker's Office in the rotunda.

Top: The dome and the roof of the Assembly.
Middle: The east wing of the Legislature in fall.
Left: The south grounds and staircase.

HALLWAY GALLERY

Portraits of the province's Lieutenant-Governors, Premiers and Speakers are on display on the third and fourth floors. You won't find portraits of Lieutenant-Governor Helen Hunley, Speaker David Carter and Premier Don Getty among the collection. It's considered bad luck to have your portrait hung while you are still in office. Portraits of the previous Lieutenant-Governor, Frank Lynch-Staunton and the previous Speaker, Gerard Amerongen, will join the other portraits on the seventy-fifth anniversary of the Legislature, September 3rd, 1987.

More than forty portraits are on display in the hallway galleries from a total of 100 protraits painted since the Legislature opened. Some are in other provincial buildings but a few have been rejected by the subjects and are kept from public view in government vaults. A Vancouver artist, Victor Albert Long, produced twenty-five paintings from 1911 to 1921. Another fourteen artists painted twenty-one portraits. Thirty more were commissioned during the 1970s to complete the collection.

Top left: The dome is carefully monitored for reactions to moisture and temperature extremes.
Top and middle right: The elegant Legislature Library serves communities throughout Alberta.
Right: Portraits of Lieutenant-Governors, Premiers, and Speakers hang in the galleries on the third and fourth floors.

BUMPS IN THE NIGHT

The Legislature serves another function. It's Edmonton's largest apartment block, with one difference. The massive building has only one suite and a part time resident. The Speaker doesn't hold the title to the Legislature, but in a real sense it is his or her castle. Following the practice of former Speakers, David Carter is responsible for the building.

A small suite was set aside on the fourth floor for the Speaker's use in the days when transportation was difficult and hotel accommodation not always readily available. Speaker Carter, who lives in Calgary, uses the suite occasionally. When you're the only tenant, there's no worry about noisy parties keeping you awake. But wouldn't you know that someone would install a fan next to the Speaker's suite to drone steadily through the night?

The suite is used mainly by the Speaker to receive members of the Royal Family, Governors General, parliamentarians, ambassadors and other distinguished visitors. It's an opportunity for guests making courtesy calls to the Legislature to relax with a cup of tea, sign the guest book and receive a presentation in the name of Albertans.

Is there a permanent guest, who, in the best tradition of old buildings, roams the hallways late at night? Some people insist a ghost haunts the Carillon Room on the fifth floor and occasionally ventures forth. Perhaps there is a former member with one more speech to make, searching in vain for someone to listen and applaud.

The Sergeant-at-Arms, Oscar Lacombe, downplays the ghost story. He claimed the spirit was created, probably by members of the staff in the Legislature, to frighten a nervous security guard on duty during the spooky night hours. "You hear strange creaks and groans in an old building like this."

Sure you do. But then again...

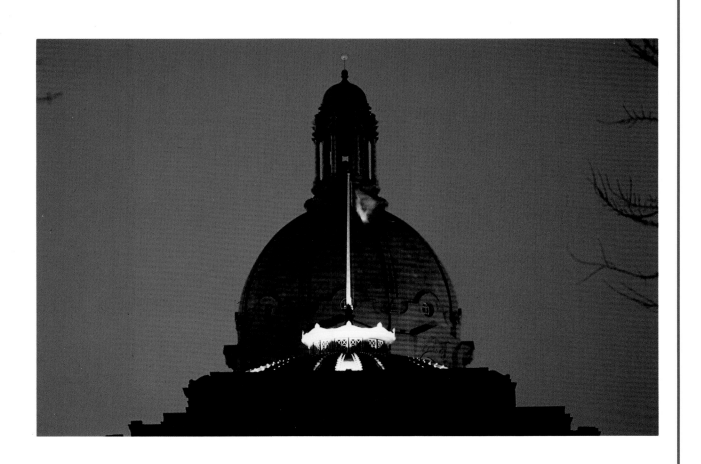

APPENDICES

LIEUTENANT GOVERNORS OF ALBERTA

Honourable George Hedley Vicars Bulyea	1905 - 1915
Honourable Robert George Brett	1915 - 1925
Honourable William Egbert	1925 - 1931
Honourable William Legh Walsh	1931 - 1936
Honourable Philip Carteret Hill Primrose	1936 - 1937
Honourable Colonel John Campbell Bowen	1937 - 1950
Honourable John James Bowlen	1950 - 1959
Honourable J. Percy Page	1959 - 1966
Honourable John Walter Grant MacEwan	1966 - 1974
Honourable Ralph Garvin Steinhauer	1974 - 1979
Honourable Frank C. Lynch-Staunton	1979 - 1984
Honourable W. Helen Hunley	1984 -

PREMIERS OF ALBERTA

Honourable Alexander C. Rutherford	1905 - 1910
Honourable Arthur Sifton	1910 - 1917
Honourable Charles Stewart	1917 - 1921
Honourable Herbert Greenfield	1921 - 1925
Honourable John E. Brownlee	1925 - 1934
Honourable Richard G. Reid	1934 - 1935
Honourable William Aberhart	1935 - 1943
Honourable Ernest C. Manning	1943 - 1968
Honourable Harry E. Strom	1968 - 1971
Honourable E. Peter Lougheed	1971 - 1985
Honourable Donald R. Getty	1985 -

LEADERS OF THE OPPOSITION OF ALBERTA

A.J. Robertson	1905 - 1909	J.P. Page	1944 - 1948
R.B. Bennett	1909 - 1910	J.H. Prowse	1948 - 1958
E. Michener	1910 - 1917	J.W.G. MacEwan	1954 - 1959
G. Hoadley	1917 - 1920	No Leader of the Opposition formally recognized	1959 - 1963
J. Ramsey	1920 - 1921	M. Maccagno	1963 - 1967
A.F. Ewing	1921	E.P. Lougheed	1967 - 1971
J.R. Boyle	1921 - 1924	H.E. Strom (1st session) J.D. Henderson (2nd session) R.C. Clark (3rd and 4th sessions)	1971 - 1975
C.R. Mitchell	1924 - 1926		
J.C. Bowen	1926	R.C. Clark	1975 - 1980
No Leader of the Opposition formally recognized	1926 - 1940	R.A. Speaker	1980 - 1982
J.H. Walker (1st and 4th sessions) A. Speakman (2nd session) J.C. Mahaffy (3rd session)	1940 - 1944	W.G. Notley	1982 - 1985
		R. Martin	1985 -

SPEAKERS OF THE LEGISLATIVE ASSEMBLY

Honourable Charles W. Fisher
(Cochrane)   March 15, 1906 - May 5, 1919
Honourable Charles S. Pingle
(Medicine Hat)   February 17, 1920 - February 1, 1922
Honourable Oran L. McPherson
(Little Bow)   December 31, 1922 - July 13, 1926
Honourable George N. Johnston
(Coronation)   February 10, 1927 - February 5, 1936
Honourable Nathan E. Tanner
(Cardston)   February 6, 1936 - January 4, 1937
Honourable Peter Dawson
(Little Bow)   February 25, 1937 - March 24, 1963
Honourable Arthur J. Dixon
(Calgary-Millican)   March 26, 1963 - March 1, 1972
Honourable Gerard J. Amerongen
(Edmonton-Meadowlark)   March 2, 1972 - June 11, 1986
Honourable David J. Carter
(Calgary-Egmont)   June 12, 1986 -

DEPUTY SPEAKERS OF THE LEGISLATIVE ASSEMBLY

John R. Boyle (Sturgeon)	1906 - 1909
John A. Simpson (Innisfail)	1910 - 1913
Joseph E. Stauffer (Didsbury)	1913 - 1916
George P. Smith (Camrose)	1917
Martin Woolf (Cardston)	1918 - 1921
Charles M. McKeen (Lac Ste. Anne)	1922 - 1935
Joseph L.P. Maynard (St. Albert)	1936
Roy C. Taylor (Pincher Creek)	1937 - 1940
Alfred J. Hooke (Rocky Mountain House)	1941
James Hartley (Macleod)	1942 - 1955
Honourable Arthur J. Dixon (Calgary-Millican)	1956 - 1963
Ashley H.C. Cooper (Vermilion-Viking)	1964 - 1971
Bill W. Diachuk (Edmonton-Beverly)	1972 - 1974
Dr. Donald J. McCrimmon (Ponoka)	1975 - 1978
Frank P. Appleby (Athabasca)	1979 - 1986
John Gogo (Lethbridge-West)	1986 -

LEGISLATIVE ASSEMBLIES OF THE PROVINCE OF ALBERTA

First Legislature	1905 - 1909
Second Legislature	1909 - 1913
Third Legislature	1913 - 1917
Fourth Legislature	1917 - 1921
Fifth Legislature	1921 - 1926
Sixth Legislature	1926 - 1930
Seventh Legislature	1930 - 1935
Eighth Legislature	1935 - 1940
Ninth Legislature	1940 - 1944
Tenth Legislature	1944 - 1948
Eleventh Legislature	1948 - 1952
Twelfth Legislature	1952 - 1955
Thirteenth Legislature	1955 - 1959
Fourteenth Legislature	1959 - 1963
Fifteenth Legislature	1963 - 1967
Sixteenth Legislature	1967 - 1971
Seventeenth Legislature	1971 - 1975
Eighteenth Legislature	1975 - 1979
Nineteenth Legislature	1979 - 1982
Twentieth Legislature	1982 - 1986
Twenty-first Legislature	1986 -

MEMBERS OF THE LEGISLATIVE ASSEMBLY OF ALBERTA, 1905-1987

Legend

Con. - Conservative
P.C. - Progressive Conservative
U.F.A. - United Farmers of Alberta
S.C. - Social Credit
N.D. - New Democratic
C.C.F. - Cooperative Commonwealth Federation
Ind. - Independent
Lib. - Liberal
Rep. - Representative
W.C.C. - Western Canada Concept
B - By-election

Name	Party	Constituency	First Legislature Elected
Anders O. Aalborg	S.C.	Alexandra	11th
William Aberhart	S.C.	Calgary	8th
J. Allen Adair	P.C.	Peace River	17th
Clayton Adams	S.C.	Edmonton	11th
Jack Ady	P.C.	Cardston	21st
Keith Alexander	P.C.	Edmonton-Whitemud	20th
Harry Alger	P.C.	Highwood	20th
Hugh W. Allen	U.F.A.	Grande Prairie	6th
Antonio Aloisio	S.C.	Athabasca	12th
Gerard J. Amerongen	P.C.	Edmonton-Meadowlark	17th
Charles E. Anderson	P.C.	St. Paul	19th
Dennis L. Anderson	P.C.	Calgary-Currie	19th
Frederic Anderson	S.C.	Calgary	8th
John V. Anderson	S.C.	Lethbridge-East	17th
Albert G. Andrews	U.F.A.	Sedgewick	5th
Ronald E. Ansley	S.C.	Leduc	8th
Frank P. Appleby	P.C.	Athabasca	17th
Frederick W. Archer	Con.	Innisfail	3rd
Herbert J. Ash	S.C.	Olds	8th
John G. Ashton	P.C.	Edmonton-Ottewell	17th
Henry B. Atkins	Lib.	Didsbury	4th
William A. Atkinson	Con.	Edmonton	7th
Winston O. Backus	P.C.	Grande Prairie	17th
William H. Bailey	U.F.A.	Peace River	7th
Floyd M. Baker	S.C.	Clover Bar	8th
Percival Baker	U.F.A.	Ponoka	5th
Perren E. Baker	U.F.A.	Medicine Hat, Cypress	5th
George R. Barker	Con.	Lac Ste. Anne	4th
Samuel A. Barnes	S.C.	Edmonton	8th
Pamela Barrett	N.D.	Edmonton-Highlands	21st
Dennis Barton	S.C.	Lesser Slave Lake	17th
John S. Batiuk	P.C.	Vegreville	17th
Joseph W. Beaudry	S.C.	St. Paul	8th
George E. Bell	S.C.	Gleichen	10th
Richard B. Bennett	Con.	Calgary	2nd
Edward P. Benoit	S.C.	Okotoks-High River Highwood	15th
Selmer A. Berg	S.C.	Alexandra	8th
Nancy Betkowski	P.C.	Edmonton-Glenora	21st
Thomas H. Blow	Con.	Calgary-South	3rd
Albert L. Blue	S.C.	Ribstone	8th
Robert Bogle	P.C.	Taber-Warner	18th

Name	Party	Constituency	First Legislature Elected
Elmer E. Borstad	P.C.	Grande Prairie	19th
Harvey Bossenberry	Lib.	Pincher Creek	7th
Lucien Boudreau	Lib.	St. Albert	2nd
Albert V. Bourcier	S.C.	Lac Ste. Anne	8th
Damase D. Bouvier	S.C.	Lac La Biche-McMurray	16th
John C. Bowen	Lib.	Edmonton	5th
John J. Bowlen	Lib.	Calgary	7th
John R. Boyle	Lib.	Sturgeon	1st
Frederick D. Bradley	P.C.	Pincher Creek	18th
Alwyn Bramley-Moore	Lib.	Alexandra	2nd
Roy Brassard	P.C.	Olds-Didsbury	21st
Paul R. Brecken	Con.	Calgary	12th
William F. Bredin	Lib.	Athabasca	1st
Douglas C. Breton	U.F.A.	Leduc	6th
Thomas A. Brick	Lib.	Peace River	1st
John T. Broomfield	Ind.	Okotoks-High River	9th
Ernest M. Brown	Ind.	Didsbury	9th
Harry K. Brown	S.C.	Pembina	8th
Samuel Brown	U.F.A.	High River	5th
John E. Brownlee	U.F.A.	Ponoka	5th
William A. Buchanan	Lib.	Lethbridge City	2nd
Walter A. Buck	S.C./Ind./Rep.	Clover Bar	16th
John C. Buckley	U.F.A.	Gleichen	5th
Leighton E. Buckwell	S.C.	Macleod	16th
Alvin F. Bullock	S.C.	Cardston	16th
John E. Butler	P.C.	Hanna-Oyen	18th
Wilson E. Cain	S.C.	Bow Valley-Empress	8th
Samuel W. Calvert	S.C.	Victoria	8th
Donald Cameron	U.F.A.	Innisfail	5th
Archie Campbell	Lib.	Vermilion	2nd
Murray J. Campbell	P.C.	Rocky Mountain House	19th
Peter M. Campbell	Unity,Ind.	Lethbridge	8th
Robert E. Campbell	Ind.	Rocky Mountain House	3rd
William A. Campbell	Lib.	Ponoka	2nd
Samuel A. Carson	U.F.A.	Sturgeon	5th
David J. Carter	P.C.	Calgary-Millican, Calgary-Egmont	19th
Ivan Casey	S.C.	Okotoks-High River	10th
Stan Cassin	P.C.	Calgary-Northwest	21st
Peter Chaba	S.C.	Redwater	11th
Thomas W. Chambers	P.C.	Edmonton-Calder	17th
William N. Chant	S.C.	Camrose	8th
Doug Cherry	P.C.	Lloydminster	21st
Catherine Chichak	P.C.	Edmonton-Norwood	17th
Mike Chornohus	U.F.A.	Whitford	5th
Philip M. Christophers	Labour	Rocky Mountain House	5th
Sheldon Chumir	Lib.	Calgary-Buffalo	21st
John E. Clark	S.C.	Stettler	12th
Lewis M. Clark	P.C.	Drumheller	19th
Robert C. Clark	S.C.	Olds-Didsbury	14th
Austin B. Claypool	U.F.A.	Didsbury	5th
Glen Clegg	P.C.	Dunvegan	21st
Charles Cockroft	S.C.	Stettler	8th
Frederick C. Colborne	S.C.	Calgary-Centre	11th
Maurice J. Conner	U.F.A.	Warner	5th
Earle G. Cook	U.F.A.	Pincher Creek	5th
Norman Cook	S.C.	Olds	9th
Roland D. B. Cook	P.C.	Edmonton-Glengarry	19th
John W. Cookson	P.C.	Lacombe	17th
Ashley H. Cooper	S.C.	Vermilion-Viking	14th
Clarence Copithorne	P.C.	Banff-Cochrane	16th
William R. Cornish	S.C.	Vermilion	10th
James K. Cornwall	Lib./Ind.	Peace River	2nd
Jean L. Cote	Lib.	Grouard	2nd
Herbert H. Crawford	Con.	Edmonton	3rd
Neil S. Crawford	P.C.	Edmonton-Parkallen	17th
Shirley A. Cripps	P.C.	Drayton Valley	19th
Charles W. Cross	Lib.	Edson	1st
Wallace W. Cross	S.C.	Hand Hills	8th
George E. Cruickshank	Ind.	Rocky Mountain House	7th
Charles O. Cunningham	Con.	Ponoka	4th
William H. Cushing	Lib.	Calgary	1st
Henry H. Dakin	Lib.	Beaver River	7th
Roy L. Davidson	S.C.	Three Hills	15th
William M. Davidson	Ind.	Calgary-North	4th
Fred Davis	Ind.	Gleichen	4th
Andrew Davison	Ind.	Calgary	9th
Peter Dawson	S.C.	Little Bow	8th
Stockwell Day	P.C.	Red Deer-North	21st
Leverett G. DeVeber	Lib.	Lethbridge	1st
Henry E. Debolt	S.C.	Spirit River	9th
Joseph M. Dechene	Lib.	Beaver River, St.Paul	5th
William Delday	S.C.	Bow Valley-Empress	14th
John A. Delisle	U.F.A.	Beaver River	6th
Joseph R. Desfosses	Lib.	Grouard	11th
Bill W. Diachuk	P.C.	Edmonton-Beverly	17th
William D. Dickie	Lib./P.C.	Calgary-Glenmore	15th
James Dinning	P.C.	Calgary-Shaw	21st
Arthur J. Dixon	S.C.	Calgary, Calgary SE, Calgary S, Calgary-Millican	12th
Clifford L. Doan	P.C.	Innisfail	17th
Thomas C. Donnelly	P.C.	Calgary-Millican	18th
Robert W. Dowling	P.C.	Edson	16th
Brian Downey	P.C.	Stettler	21st
Charles D. Drain	S.C.	Pincher Creek-Crowsnest	16th
John Drobot	P.C.	St. Paul	20th
John Dubetz	S.C.	Redwater	14th
David M. Duggan	Con.	Edmonton	6th
Lawrence E. O. Duke	S.C.	Rocky Mountain House Pincher Creek-Crowsnest	8th
Nick W. Dushenski	C.C.F.	Willingdon	12th
Robert B. Eaton	Lib.	Hand Hills	3rd
Arthur W. Ebbett	Lib.	Vermilion	4th
Robert C. Edwards	Ind.	Calgary	5th
Robert Elliott	P.C.	Grande Prairie	20th
Ross L. Ellis	Lib./Con.	Okotoks-High River	13th
Roy B. Ells	S.C.	Grouard	14th
Peter Elzinga	P.C.	Sherwood Park	21st
Sheila B. Embury	P.C.	Calgary-Northwest	19th
Peter J. Enzenauer	U.F.A.	Alexandra	5th
Harry K. Everitt	S.C.	St. Albert	14th
Ed Ewasiuk	N.D.	Edmonton-Beverly	21st
Albert F. Ewing	Con.	Edmonton-West	4th
Frank R. Falconer	Lib.	Athabasca	7th
William A. Fallow	S.C.	Vermilion, Grouard	8th
William G. Farquharson	U.F.A.	Ribstone	5th
Roy A. Farran	P.C.	Calgary-North Hill	17th
Hugh C. Farthing	Con.	Calgary	7th
William Fedun	U.F.A.	Victoria	5th
Albert E. Fee	S.C.	Sedgewick	8th
Adolph O. Fimrite	S.C.	Spirit River	12th
William T. Finlay	Lib.	Medicine Hat	1st
Robert Fischer	P.C.	Wainwright	20th
Charles W. Fisher	Lib.	Cochrane	1st
E. LeRoy Fjordbotten	P.C.	Macleod	19th
August W. Flamme	S.C.	Cypress	8th
Donald S. Flemming	S.C.	Calgary-West	14th
Allison I. Fluker	P.C.	St. Paul	17th
Gordon A. Forster	U.F.A.	Hand Hills	5th
Edward P. Foster	S.C.	Didsbury	8th
James L. Foster	P.C.	Red Deer	17th
Derek Fox	N.D.	Vegreville	21st
John W. Frame	Lib.	Athabasca	6th
Clinton K. French	S.C.	Hand Hills, Hand Hills-Acadia, Hanna-Oyen	14th
Myrna C. Fyfe	P.C.	St. Albert	19th
John J. Gaetz	Lib.	Red Deer	4th
Francis L. Gainer	Coalition	Banff-Cochrane	13th
Daniel H. Galbraith	U.F.A.	Nanton	5th
Wilfrid Gariepy	Lib.	Beaver River	3rd
Stanley G. Geldart	S.C.	Edmonton-West	15th
Colin M. Genge	Lib.	Macleod	2nd
Clarence E. Gerhart	S.C.	Acadia-Coronation	9th
Edgar H. Gerhart	S.C.	Edmonton, Edmonton-Northwest	12th
Donald R. Getty	P.C.	Edmonton, Strathcona-West, Edmonton-Whitemud	16th
Ronald D. Ghitter	P.C.	Calgary-Buffalo	17th
Charles L. Gibbs	Labour	Edmonton	6th
Gerry Gibeault	N.D.	Edmonton-Millwoods	21st
William F. Gilliland	S.C.	Peace River	10th
Andrew Gilmour	Con.	Lacombe	4th
Leonidas A. Giroux	Lib.	Grouard	5th
John M. Glendenning	Lib.	Nanton	2nd
John A. Gogo	P.C.	Lethbridge	18th
Alexander W. Gordey	S.C.	Vegreville-Bruce	14th
Isidore Goresky	U.F.A.	Whitford	7th
Edith H. Gostick	S.C.	Calgary	8th
Edward L. Gray	Lib.	Edmonton	8th
Herbert Greenfield	U.F.A.	Peace River	5th
Frank S. Grisdale	U.F.A.	Olds	7th
Richard D. Gruenwald	S.C.	Lethbridge-West	17th
Peter Gunn	Lib.	Lac Ste. Anne	2nd

Name	Party	Constituency	First Legislature Elected	Name	Party	Constituency	First Legislature Elected
James Gurnett	N.D.	Spirit River-Fairview	20th	Henry Kroeger	P.C.	Sedgewick-Coronation	
Richard E. Hall	Lib.	Athabasca	13th			Chinook	18th
Leonard C. Halmrast	S.C.	Warner, Taber-		John Kushner	P.C.	Calgary-Mountain View	18th
		Warner	10th	Stanley A. Kushner	P.C.	Calgary-Mountain View	19th
Howard G. Hammell	S.C.	Didsbury	10th	Marie Laing	N.D.	Edmonton-Avonmore	21st
Ernest G. Hansell	S.C.	Okotoks-High River	14th	Romeo B. Lamothe	S.C.	Bonnyville	14th
Donald A. Hansen	P.C.	Bonnyville	17th	William J. Lampley	S.C.	Peace River	8th
James Hansen	S.C.	Taber	8th	John C. Landeryou	S.C.	Lethbridge	10th
Earl M. Hardy	S.C.	Bruce	11th	George Lane	Lib.	Bow Valley	3rd
Graham L. Harle	P.C.	Stettler	17th	Hector Lang	Lib.	Medicine Hat	6th
James Hartley	S.C.	Macleod	8th	Frank Laut	Ind.	Banff-Cochrane	9th
Harry O. Haslam	S.C.	Nanton-Claresholm	8th	Mary J. LeMessurier	P.C.	Edmonton-Centre	19th
Bob Hawkesworth	N.D.	Calgary-Mountain View	21st	Lorne L. Leavitt	S.C.	Calgary-	
William E. Hayes	S.C.	Stony Plain	8th			Queen's Park	15th
Louis W. Heard	S.C.	Edmonton-Northeast	14th	Brian Lee	P.C.	Calgary-Buffalo	20th
Jeremiah W. Heffernan	Lib.	Edmonton	5th	Calvin E. Lee	P.C.	Calgary-McKnight	17th
James D. Henderson	S.C./Ind.	Leduc, Wetaskiwin-		Ernest L. Lee	S.C.	Dunvegan	15th
		Leduc	15th	Roy S. Lee	S.C.	Taber	9th
Rudolph Hennig	U.F.A.	Clover Bar	6th	William G. Lee	S.C.	Athabasca	9th
William T. Henry	Lib.	Edmonton	5th	Frank S. Leffingwell	Lib.	Warner	3rd
Jim Heron	P.C.	Stony Plain	21st	Harry C. Leinweber	S.C.	Medicine Hat	14th
Elizabeth J. Hewes	Lib.	Edmonton-Gold Bar	21st	Clarence M. Leitch	P.C.	Calgary-Egmont	17th
Alois P. Hiebert	P.C.	Edmonton-Gold Bar	19th	Prosper E. Lessard	Lib.	St. Paul	2nd
Cornelius Hiebert	Con.	Rosebud	1st	Alymer J.E. Liesemer	C.C.F.	Calgary	10th
John C. Hillman	S.C.	Sedgewick-Coronation	12th	Andrew Little	P.C.	Calgary-McCall	18th
Samuel B. Hillocks	Con.	Calgary-North	3rd	Harry Lobay	S.C.	Beaver River	
Norman Hindsley	Ind.	Calgary	7th			Lac La Biche	11th
Edgar Hinman	S.C.	Cardston	12th	E. Peter Lougheed	P.C.	Calgary-West	16th
George Ho Lem	S.C.	Calgary-McCall	17th	John R. Love	U.F.A.	Wainwright	5th
George Hoadley	Con.	Okotoks-High River	2nd	Solon E. Low	S.C.	Warner	8th
Albert E. Hohol	P.C.	Edmonton-Belmont	17th	James R. Lowery	Con.	Alexandra	3rd
James B. Holden	Lib.	Vermilion	1st	Albert W. Ludwig	S.C.	Calgary-Northeast	
Charles G. Holder	S.C.	St. Albert	8th			Calgary-East	
Ambrose Holowach	S.C.	Edmonton-Centre	14th			Calgary-Mountain View	14th
Alfred J. Hooke	S.C.	Red Deer		Frederick W. Lundy	Con.	Stony Plain	4th
		Rocky Mountain House	8th	David Lush	S.C.	Empress	8th
John W. Horan	S.C.	Edmonton-Jasper Place	15th	Joseph F. Lymburn	U.F.A.	Edmonton	6th
Hugh M. Horner	P.C.	Lac Ste. Anne		Thomas F.L. Lysons	P.C.	Vermilion-Viking	18th
		Barrhead	16th	Roberta C. MacAdam	Soldiers	Province at Large	4th
James D. Horsman	P.C.	Medicine Hat-Redcliff		Gordon MacDonald	Lib.	Pembina	3rd
		Medicine Hat	18th	Howard B. MacDonald	Ind./S.C.	Calgary	10th
William R. Howson	Lib.	Edmonton	7th	Hugh J. MacDonald	Lib.	Calgary	11th
George L. Hudson	Con.	Wainwright	3rd	Hugh J. MacDonald	Ind.	Edmonton	9th
John William Hugill	S.C.	Calgary	8th	J. W. Grant MacEwan	Lib.	Calgary	13th
W. Helen Hunley	P.C.	Rocky Mountain House	17th	Alexander G. MacKay	Lib.	Athabasca	3rd
Alan W. Hyland	P.C.	Cypress		John Mackintosh	Ind.	Bow Valley	7th
		Cypress-Redcliff	18th	George MacLauchlan	U.F.A./Ind.	Pembina	5th
Louis D. Hyndman	P.C.	Edmonton-West		Glenwell L. MacLachlan	S.C.	Coronation	8th
		Edmonton-Glenora	16th	Roderick A. MacLeod	S.C.	Olds	13th
Herbert Ingrey	S.C.	Drumheller	8th	Duncan B. MacMillan	S.C.	Lacombe	8th
John Irwin	Con.	Calgary	6th	Michael Maccagno	Lib.	Lac La Biche	13th
Ernest D. Isley	P.C.	Bonnyville	19th	William L. Mack	P.C.	Edmonton-Belmont	19th
Fay D. Jackson	Ind.	Cypress	9th	William S. Mackie	S.C.	Stettler	10th
Norman B. James	S.C.	Acadia, Edmonton	8th	A. Erskin Maclellan	S.C.	Innisfail	8th
Frederick C. Jamieson	Con.	Edmonton	7th	John J. MacLellan	U.F.A.	Taber	7th
Richard H. Jamieson	S.C.	Jasper-West	14th	Alfred Macyk	Lib.	Redwater	13th
William E. Jamison	P.C.	St. Albert	17th	Norman F. Magee	P.C.	Red Deer	19th
Ralph A. Jespersen	S.C.	Stony Plain	16th	James C. Mahaffy	Ind.	Calgary	9th
A. Dick Johnston	P.C.	Lethbridge-East	18th	Frederick T. Mandeville	S.C.	Bow Valley-Empress	16th
Charles E. Johnston	S.C.	Calgary-Bowness	14th	Ernest C. Manning	S.C.	Calgary, Edmonton	
George N. Johnston	U.F.A.	Coronation	5th			Strathcona-East	8th
Glen F. Johnston	S.C.	Ponoka	12th	John P. Marcellus	Lib.	Pincher Creek	1st
William G. Johnston	Dom.			Duncan M. Marshall	Lib.	Olds	2nd
	Labour	Medicine Hat	5th	Robert C. Marshall	Lib.	Calgary	5th
Laudas Joly	S.C.	St. Paul, Bonnyville	5th	Eld J. Martin	Ind.	Peace River	9th
Halvar Jonson	P.C.	Ponoka,		Ray Martin	N.D.	Edmonton-Norwood	20th
		Ponoka-Rimbey	20th	William Masson	S.C.	Wainwright	8th
Robin D. Jorgenson	S.C.	Pembina	10th	Archie M. Matheson	U.F.A.	Vegreville	5th
Jake H. Josvanger	Lib.	Bonnyville	13th	Joseph L.P. Maynard	S.C.	Beaver River, St. Albert	8th
Marion A. Kelts	S.C.	Acadia-Coronation	14th	A.J. McArthur	Lib.	Gleichen	2nd
John H.W.S. Kemmis	Con.	Pincher Creek	2nd	John P. McArthur	Lib.	Gleichen	3rd
Donald M. Kennedy	U.F.A.	Peace River	5th	Joseph S. McCallum	Lib.	Vegreville	3rd
Gordon L. Kesler	W.C.C.	Olds-Didsbury	19th(B)	Matthew McCauley	Lib.	Vermilion	1st
Frederick A. Kidd	P.C.	Banff	18th	Nellie L. McClung	Lib.	Edmonton	5th
David T. King	P.C.	Edmonton-Highlands	17th	John A. McColl	Lib.	Acadia	3rd
William R. King	S.C.	Cochrane	8th	Robert M. McCool	U.F.A.	Cochrane	6th
William J.C. Kirby	P.C.	Red Deer	12th	Elaine McCoy	P.C.	Calgary-West	21st
Peter Knaak	P.C.	Edmonton-Whitemud	19th	Stewart A. McCrae	P.C.	Calgary-Foothills	18th
Janet Koper	P.C.	Calgary-Foothills	20th	Donald J. McCrimmon	P.C.	Ponoka	17th
William A. Kovach	S.C.	Pincher Creek-		Isaac M. McCune	S.C.	Gleichen	8th
		Crowsnest	11th	John A. McDougall	Lib.	Edmonton	2nd
Kenneth R. Kowalski	P.C.	Barrhead	19th	Alex McEachern	N.D.	Edmonton-Kingsway	21st
Julian G.J. Koziak	P.C.	Edmonton-Strathcona	17th	Harold W. McGill	Con.	Calgary	7th

Name	Party	Constituency	First Legislature Elected
Alexander A. McGillivray	Con.	Calgary	6th
Charles M. McKeen	U.F.A.	Lac Ste. Anne	5th
Percy A. McKelvey	Ind.	Ponoka	9th
Henry W. McKenny	Lib.	Clearwater	1st
Malcolm McKenzie	Lib.	Macleod, Claresholm	1st
Louise C. McKinney	U.F.A.	Claresholm	4th
Donald J. McKinnon	Ind.	Gleichen	9th
Randolph H. McKinnon	S.C.	Strathcona-West	14th
Ira McLaughlin	S.C.	Grande Prairie	10th
John H. McLaughlin	Lib.	Stony Plain	13th
Archibald J. McLean	Ind./Lib.	Taber	2nd
Andrew R. McLennan	Lib.	Edmonton	5th
Donald McLeod	U.F.A.	Stony Plain	7th
John R. McLeod	Lib.	Ponoka	1st
Donald McNabb	Labour	Lethbridge	1st
James McNaughton	Lib.	Little Bow	3rd
James L. McPherson	S.C.	Vegreville, Bruce	8th
James R. McPherson	P.C.	Red Deer	20th
John A. McPherson	Lib.	Stony Plain	1st
O.L. "Tony" McPherson	U.F.A.	Little Bow	5th
Nicholas A. Melnyk	S.C.	Willingdon-Two Hills	14th
L. Petrie Meston	S.C.	Three Hills	15th
Edward Michener	Ind./Con.	Red Deer	2nd
George M. Milhalcheon	U.F.A.	Whitford	6th
Abe W. Miller	Lib.	Edmonton	13th
Douglas Miller	S.C.	Taber-Warner	16th
James E. Miller	P.C.	Lloydminster	17th
George Mills	Ind./Lib.	Athabasca	4th
John A. Mills	Lib.	Lac Ste. Anne	13th
Thomas C. Milnes	Lib.	Claresholm	5th
Gordon T.W. Miniely	P.C.	Edmonton-Centre	17th
Dianne Mirosh	P.C.	Calgary-Glenmore	21st
Peter A. Miskiw	U.F.A.	Victoria	7th
Arthur P. Mitchell	Lib.	Leduc	7th
Charles R. Mitchell	Lib.	Bow Valley	2nd
Grant Mitchell	Lib.	Edmonton-Meadowlark	21st
Christine Mjolsness	N.D.	Edmonton-Calder	21st
William Moffat	Lib.	Claresholm	3rd
Angelo M. Montemurro	S.C.	Lac Ste. Anne	12th
Euell F. Montgomery	S.C.	Peace River	14th
Hugh J. Montgomery	Lib.	Wetaskiwin	3rd
Alexander Moore	U.F.A.	Cochrane	4th
John T. Moore	Lib.	Red Deer	1st
Marvin E. Moore	P.C.	Smoky River	17th
Ora B. Moore	S.C.	Ponoka	10th
Ronald Moore	P.C.	Lacombe	20th
Daniel J. Morkelberg	Lib.	Innisfail	4th
Walter Morrish	Lib.	Edmonton	8th
A.J. Morrison	Labour	Edson	9th
William Morrison	S.C.	Okotoks-High River	8th
Frederick C. Moyer	Ind.	Drumheller	7th
David B. Mullen	S.C.	Camrose, Edmonton	8th
Carl Muller	S.C.	Pembina	16th
Eric W.C. Musgrave	P.C.	Calgary-McKnight	18th
Tom Musgrove	P.C.	Bow Valley	20th
Stan Nelson	P.C.	Calgary-McCall	20th
Frederick J. Niddrie	S.C.	Olds	11th
Karl E. Nordstrom	S.C.	Bonnyville	14th
Galen C. Norris	S.C.	Stettler	13(B)
W. Grant Notley	N.D.	Spirit River-Fairview	17th
Charles M. O'Brien	Socialist	Rocky Mountain House	2nd
L.J. O'Brien	Ind.	Grande Prairie	9th
Gerald O'Conner	Lib.	Edmonton	8th
John Oldring	P.C.	Red Deer-South	21st
Charles H. Olin	Lib.	Wetaskiwin	2nd
Edwin A. Oman	P.C.	Calgary-North Hill	19th
Rick Orman	P.C.	Calgary-Montrose	21st
Constance E. Osterman	P.C.	Three Hills	19th
James L. Owens	S.C.	Didsbury	13th
J. Percy Page	Ind./P.C.	Edmonton	10th
Milton G. Pahl	P.C.	Edmonton-Mill Woods	19th
Carl Paproski	P.C.	Edmonton-Kingsway	20th
Kenneth R.H. Paproski	P.C.	Edmonton-Kingsway	17th
Robert H. Parkyn	Ind./Labour	Calgary	6th
Mary I. Parlby	U.F.A.	Lacombe	5th
Barry Pashak	N.D.	Calgary-Forest Lawn	21st
Allen R. Patrick	S.C.	Lacombe	12th
Alphaeus Patterson	Con.	Peace River	3rd
Robert Patterson	Ind./Con.	Macleod	2nd
William Patterson	S.C.	Lac Ste. Anne	14th
Christopher Pattinson	Labour	Edson	6th
William E. Payne	P.C.	Calgary-Fish Creek	19th
William E. Payne	Con.	Red Deer	7th
Frederick H. Peacock	P.C.	Calgary-Currie	17th
Robert Pearson	Ind.	Calgary	4th
Nigelian Pengelly	P.C.	Innisfail	19th
Lawerence Peterson	U.F.A.	Taber	5th
Charles S. Pingle	Lib.	Redcliff-Medicine Hat	3rd
Leo Piquette	N.D.	Athabasca-Lac La Biche	21st
Hugh L. Planche	P.C.	Calgary-Glenmore	18th
Michael H. Ponich	S.C.	Vegreville	10th
James M. Popil	S.C.	Sturgeon, Redwater	8th
Warren W. Prevey	Lib.	Edmonton	6th
Lorne Proudfoot	U.F.A.	Acadia	5th
James H. Prowse	Lib.	Edmonton	11th
Edward H. Prudden	Lib.	Stettler	4th
William F. Puffer	Lib.	Lacombe	1st
William F. Purdy	P.C.	Stony Plain	17th
Gerrit J. Radstaak	S.C.	Strathcona-South	16th
William A. Rae	Lib.	Peace River	4th
James Ramsey	Con.	Edmonton-East	4th
Raymond S. Ratzlaff	S.C.	Three Hills	16th
Ian W.C. Reid	P.C.	Edson, West Yellowhead	19th
Richard G. Reid	U.F.A.	Vermilion	5th
Raymond Reierson	S.C.	St. Paul	12th
Chester A. Reynolds	S.C.	Stettler	9th
Ezra H. Riley	Lib.	Gleichen	1st(B)
Harold W.H. Riley	Con.	Gleichen	2nd
Louis M. Roberts	Lib.	High River	2nd
William Roberts	N.D.	Edmonton-Centre	21st
Albert J. Robertson	Con.	High River	1st
Jack G. Robertson	P.C.	Stettler	17th
Elizabeth D. Robinson	S.C.	Medicine Hat	12th
John L. Robinson	S.C.	Medicine Hat	8th
Edith B. Rogers	S.C.	Ponoka	8th
Chester A. Ronning	U.F.A.	Camrose	7th
Elmer E. Roper	C.C.F.	Edmonton	9th(B)
Neville S. Roper	S.C.	Ponoka	16th
Anthony S. Rosenroll	Lib.	Wetaskiwin	1st
Alexander Ross	Labour	Calgary	4th
Charles C. Ross	S.C.	Athabasca	8th
Joseph D. Ross	S.C.	Strathcona-Centre	12th
William H. Ross	Lib.	Calgary	7th(B)
Ken Rostad	P.C.	Camrose	21st
Dave J. Russell	P.C.	Calgary-Victoria Park, Calgary-Elbow	16th
Henry A. Ruste	S.C.	Wainwright	13th
Alexander C. Rutherford	Lib.	Strathcona	1st
Stanley N. Ruzycki	C.C.F.	Vegreville	13th
Albert L. Sanders	U.F.A.	Stettler	5th
Chester I. Sayers	S.C.	Camrose	9th(B)
Horst A.L.C. Schmid	P.C.	Edmonton-Avonmore	17th
Dallas W. Schmidt	P.C.	Wetaskiwin-Leduc	18th
Stan Schumacher	P.C.	Drumheller	21st
Joseph M. Scruggs	S.C.	Dunvegan	14th
Michael Senych	S.C.	Redwater	15th
Lawrence R. Shaben	P.C.	Lesser Slave Lake	18th
Andrew S. Shandro	Lib.	Whitford	3rd
William Sharpe	S.C.	Grande Prairie	8th
Joseph T. Shaw	Lib.	Bow Valley	6th
Robert L. Shaw	Lib.	Stettler	2nd
William H. Shield	U.F.A.	Macleod	5th
Gordon Shrake	P.C.	Calgary-Millican	20th
Arthur L. Sifton	Lib.	Vermilion	2nd
Tom Sigurdson	N.D.	Edmonton-Belmont	21st
William C. Simmons	Lib.	Lethbridge	1st(B)
John A. Simpson	Lib.	Innisfail	1st
Robert A. Simpson	S.C.	Calgary-North	15th
James L. Sims	Lib.	Acadia-Coronation	13th
Thomas L. Sindlinger	P.C.	Calgary-Buffalo	19th
George Skelding	Lib.	Macleod	4th
Andrew Smeaton	Labour	Lethbridge	6th
Arthur R. Smith	Con.	Calgary	13th
George P. Smith	Lib.	Camrose	2nd
George W. Smith	U.F.A.	Red Deer	5th
Nelson S. Smith	U.F.A.	Olds	5th
Vernor W. Smith	U.F.A.	Camrose	5th
William C. Smith	U.F.A.	Empress, Redcliff	5th
Arthur J. Soetaert	Lib.	St. Albert	13th
Ralph A. Sorenson	S.C.	Sedgewick-Coronation	17th
Evert E. Sparks	U.F.A.	Wetaskiwin	5th

Name	Party	Constituency	First Legislature Elected
Donald Sparrow	P.C.	Wetaskiwin-Leduc	20th
Raymond A. Speaker	S.C./Ind./Repr.	Little Bow	15th
Alfred Speakman	Ind.	Red Deer	9th
Nelson Spencer	Con.	Medicine Hat	3rd
Telesphore St. Arnaud	U.F.A.	St. Albert	5th
Omer St. Germain	U.F.A./Lib.	St. Albert	7th
George D. Stanley	Ind./Con.	High River	3rd
Joseph E. State	Lib.	Clearwater	4th
Joseph E. Stauffer	Lib.	Didsbury	2nd
Greg P. Stevens	P.C.	Banff-Cochrane	19th
Charles Stewart	P.C.	Wainwright	18th
Charles A. Stewart	Lib.	Sedgewick	2nd
Frederick A. Stewart	P.C.	Calgary-North Hill	21st
John S. Stewart	Con.	Lethbridge City	2nd
Stephen Stiles	P.C.	Olds-Didsbury	20th
Bryce C. Stringham	Ind.	Bow Valley-Empress	13th
George L. Stringham	U.F.A.	Cardston	5th
Albert W. Strohschein	S.C.	Wetaskiwin	15th
Harry E. Strom	S.C.	Cypress	13th
Gordon E. Stromberg	P.C.	Camrose	17th
Bryan Strong	N.D.	St. Albert	21st
Charles A. Stuart	Lib.	Gleichen	1st
William A. Switzer	Lib.	Edson	15th(B)
Walter Szwender	P.C.	Edmonton-Belmont	20th
Clarence Tade	S.C.	Athabasca	8th
Harold E. Tanner	Lib.	Edmonton	13th
Nathan E. Tanner	S.C.	Cardston	8th
Gordon E. Taylor	S.C./Ind.	Drumheller	9th
Nicholas W. Taylor	Lib.	Westlock-Sturgeon	21st
Roy C. Taylor	S.C.	Pincher Creek	8th
Robert T. Telford	Lib.	Leduc	1st
Lionel R. Tellier	Ind.	St.Albert	9th
Ronald J. Tesolin	P.C.	Lac La Biche-McMurray	18th
John M. Thompson	P.C.	Cardston	18th
Edith B. Thurston	S.C.	Cypress	10th
Stanley G. Tobin	Lib.	Leduc	3rd
William Tomyn	S.C.	Whitford, Willingdon, Edmonton-Norwood	8th
George Topolnisky	P.C.	Redwater-Andrew	17th
Joseph H. Tremblay	Lib.	Grouard	8th
Peter Trynchy	P.C.	Whitecourt	17th
Garth A. Turcott	N.D.	Pincher Creek-Crowsnest	15th
James G. Turgeon	Lib.	Ribstone	3rd
Thomas M.M. Tweedie	Con.	Calgary-Centre	2nd
James M. Underdahl	S.C.	Cypress	11th
Joseph H. Unwin	S.C.	Edson	8th
David A. Ure	S.C.	Red Deer	9th(B)
William K. Ure	S.C.	Red Deer	14th
George H. Van Allen	Lib.	Edmonton	8th
Francis A. Walker	Lib.	Victoria	1st
Gordon B. Walker	U.F.A.	Nanton-Claresholm	6th
James H. Walker	Ind.	Warner	9th
Thomas J.J. Walker	P.C.	Macleod	18th
Loftus D. Ward	Navy Rep. (W.W. II)		10th
David Warnock	Lib.	Pincher Creek	2nd
Allen A. Warrack	P.C.	Three Hills	17th
Willard M. Washburn	U.F.A.	Stony Plain	5th
Ernest S. Watkins	P.C.	Calgary-Glenmore	13th
Charles Y. Weaver	Con.	Edmonton	6th
P. Neil Webber	P.C.	Calgary-Bow	18th
George H. Webster	Lib.	Calgary	6th
Conrad Weidenhammer	Con.	Stony Plain	3rd
James Weir	Ind.	Nanton	4th
Norman A. Weiss	P.C.	Lac La Biche-McMurray Fort McMurray	19th
Leonard F. Werry	P.C.	Calgary-Foothills, Calgary-Bowness	16th
Steven West	P.C.	Vermilion-Viking	21st
Fred J. White	Labour	Calgary	5th
Frank H. Whiteside	Lib.	Coronation	3rd
Russell J. Whitson	Lib.	Vermilion	13th
Robert H. Wiebe	S.C.	Peace River	16th
Hans E. Wight	S.C.	Lethbridge	8th
Rose Wilkinson	S.C.	Calgary-North	10th
William J. Williams	Vet. & Active Force	Edmonton	10th
Norman A. Willmore	S.C.	Edson	10th
Ethel S. Wilson	S.C.	Edmonton-North	14th
Roy G. Wilson	S.C.	Calgary-Bow	17th
William W. Wilson	Con.	Coronation	4th
John A. Wingblade	S.C.	Wetaskiwin	8th
George K. Wolstenholme	P.C.	Highwood	18th
Henry Woo	P.C.	Sherwood Park	19th
Cornelia L.R. Wood	S.C.	Stony Plain	9th
John B.T. Wood	S.C.	Grouard	11th
John W. Woolf	Lib.	Cardston	1st
Martin Woolf	Lib.	Cardston	2nd(B)
George Woytkiw	S.C.	Vegreville	9th
Arthur H. Wray	S.C./Ind.	Banff-Cochrane	10th
Charles O.F. Wright	U.F.A.	Ribstone	5th
Gordon Wright	N.D.	Edmonton-Strathcona	21st
William R. Wyse	S.C.	Medicine Hat-Redcliff	17th
Leslie G. Young	P.C.	Edmonton-Jasper Place	17th
John Younie	N.D.	Edmonton-Glengarry	21st
William J. Yurko	P.C.	Edmonton-Gold Bar	16th
Rudolph Zander	P.C.	Drayton Valley	17th
John B. Zaozirny	P.C.	Calgary-Forest Lawn	19th
Steve Zarusky	P.C.	Redwater-Andrew	21st
Bohdan Zip	P.C.	Calgary-Mountain View	20th

BIBLIOGRAPHY

Barr, John J. *The Dynasty: The Rise and Fall of Social Credit in Alberta*. Toronto: McClelland and Stewart Limited, 1974.

Calderola, Carlo. *Society and Politics in Alberta: Research Papers*. Agincourt, Ont.: Methuen, 1979.

Articles used from the above collection include:

Lewis Thomas, ''The Liberal Party in Alberta, 1905 - 1921''

Carl Betke, ''The United Farmers of Alberta, 1921 - 1935''

Cook Duggan, Grace. *Roots and Romance: The David and Marion Duggan Family*. Edmonton. n.d.

Easterbrook, W.T. Aitken, Hugh G.J. *Canadian Economic History*. Toronto: The Macmillan Company of Canada Limited, 1956.

Fryer, Harold. *Alberta - The Pioneer Years*. Langley, B.C.: Sunfire, 1977.

Hooke, Alfred J. *30 + 5: I Know I Was There*. Edmonton: Institute of Applied Art, 1971.

Hustak, Allan. *Peter Lougheed: A Biography*. Toronto: McClelland and Stewart, 1979.

Irving, John A. *The Social Credit Movement in Alberta*. Toronto: The University of Toronto Press, 1939.

Kennedy, Fred. *Alberta Was My Beat: Memoirs of a Western Newspaperman*. Calgary: The Albertan, 1975.

MacEwan, Grant. *Fifty Mighty Men*. Saskatoon: Western Producer Prairie Books, 1982.

MacEwan, Grant. *Frederick Haultain*. Saskatoon: Western Producer Prairie Books, 1985.

MacDonald, Janice E. *The Northwest Fort*. Edmonton: Lone Pine Publishing, 1983.

McDougall, D.B. *A History of the Legislative Library*. Edmonton. n.d.

MacGregor, James. *A History of Alberta*. Edmonton: Hurtig, 1972.

MacInnes, C.M. *In the Shadow of the Rockies*. London: Rivingtons, 1930.

Metcalfe, William H. *The View From Thirty: A Veteran Newsman Files His Last Dispatch*. Winnipeg: Metcalfe, 1984.

Owram, Douglas. *The Formation of Alberta: A Documentary History*. Calgary: Historical Society of Alberta, 1979.

Pratt, Larry. *Socialism and Democracy in Alberta: Essays in Honour of Grant Notley*. Edmonton: NeWest Press, 1986.

Smith, Maurice Greer. *Political Organization of the Plains Indians*. New York: AMS Press, 1978.

Watkins, Ernest. *The Golden Province: A Political History of Alberta*. Calgary: Sandstone, 1980.

Wood, David G. *The Lougheed Legacy*. Key Porter Books, 1985.

Wark, Kenneth A. *A Report on Alberta Elections: 1905 - 1982*. Edmonton.

Newspapers:
Calgary *Herald*, various dates.
Edmonton *Bulletin*, various dates.
Edmonton *Journal*, various dates.
Edmonton *Saturday Evening News*, various dates.
Lethbridge *News*, various dates.
Macleod *Gazette*, various dates.

PHOTOCREDITS

Plains Publishing gratefully acknowledges the kind assistance and cooperation of the following individuals, agencies and corporations in providing the photographs which appear in this book. Entries are by page number, coded as follows: T - top; B - bottom; M - middle; C - centre; L - left; R - right; GAI - Glenbow-Alberta Institute; PAA - Provincial Archives of Alberta; PAB - Public Affairs Bureau.

Front cover: courtesy Agrapha ; back cover: courtesy PAB;

xii courtesy PAB;

1 T: E. Brown Collection, courtesy PAA (B6672); B: E. Brown Collection, courtesy PAA (B6717);

2 T: E. Brown Collection, courtesy PAA (B6731); B: courtesy GAI (NA-1030-28);

3 E. Brown Collection, courtesy PAA (B6619);

4 courtesy PAA (A10611);

5 L: courtesy Rolf Albert; R: Calgary *Eye Opener*, 1905, courtesy GAI (NA-3055-16);

6 T: courtesy Rolf Albert; B: E. Brown Collection, courtesy PAA (B6654);

7 E. Brown Collection, courtesy PAA (B6661);

8 T: E. Brown Collection, courtesy PAA (B6527); B: courtesy PAA (P5345);

9 E. Brown Collection, courtesy PAA (B6667);

10 E. Brown Collection, courtesy PAA (B6741);

11 courtesy PAA;

12 E. Brown Collection, courtesy PAA (B6736);

13 T: courtesy Travel Alberta; B: courtesy PAB;

14 Paul Kane, 1846, courtesy Stark Museum of Art;

15 T: E. Brown Collection, courtesy PAA (B7130); B: courtesy Rolf Albert;

16 courtesy PAA;

17 courtesy PAB;

18 L: Francis Dias, Camera Press London, courtesy Canapress; R: courtesy Rhode Island Department of Economic Development;

19 L: courtesy Minnesota Legislative Photo Services; R: courtesy Wisconsin Department of Tourism;

20 T: E. Brown Collection, courtesy PAA (B3356); M: E. Brown Collection, courtesy PAA (B6595); B: E. Brown Collection, courtesy PAA (B3386);

21 TL: courtesy GAI (NA-3190-1); TR: courtesy GAI (NC-6-50); B: courtesy PAB;

22 courtesy GAI (NC-6-527);

23 courtesy PAB;

24 T: courtesy PAB; B: courtesy GAI (NC-6-234);

25 T: courtesy GAI (NC-6-3238); B: courtesy PAB;

26 courtesy PAB;

27 courtesy PAB;

28 TL, TR. BL. BR: courtesy Rolf Albert;

29 T: courtesy PAB; B: courtesy Rolf Albert;

30 TL, TR, M, B: courtesy Rolf Albert;

31 TL, TR, M, B: courtesy Rolf Albert;

32 T, B: courtesy Rolf Albert;

33 TL, TR, B: courtesy Rolf Albert;

34 courtesy Rolf Albert;

35 courtesy PAB;

36 courtesy PAB;

37 T, M: courtesy PAB; B: courtesy Rolf Albert;

38 TL, TR, M, BL, BR: courtesy Rolf Albert;

39 TL, TR, ML, MR, BL, BR: courtesy Rolf Albert;

40 courtesy Rolf Albert;

41 T: courtesy PAB; BL, BR: courtesy Rolf Albert;

42 courtesy Rolf Albert;

43 T, B: courtesy Rolf Albert;

44 T: courtesy GAI; BL, BR: courtesy Rolf Albert;

45 T: courtesy PAA; BL: courtesy PAA; BR: courtesy Rolf Albert;

46 T, B: courtesy Rolf Albert;

47 courtesy PAB;

48 courtesy PAB;

49 courtesy PAB;

50 T: courtesy Rolf Albert; B: courtesy Rolf Albert;

51 courtesy Rolf Albert;

52 T, B:courtesy Rolf Albert;

53 L: courtesy PAA; R: courtesy PAB;

54 T, B: courtesy PAB;

55 courtesy PAB;

56 T, B: courtesy PAB;

57 courtesy Rolf Albert;

58 T: courtesy PAA; BL: courtesy PAA; BR: courtesy PAA;

59 T, B: courtesy Alf Hooke;

60 L: courtesy Rolf Albert; ML: courtesy PAA; B: courtesy Rolf Albert;

61 T, ML, MR, B: courtesy Rolf Albert;

62 courtesy PAA (PA5218);

63 T: courtesy PAA (J432/2); B: courtesy Rolf Albert;

64 L: courtesy PAB; TR, BR: courtesy Rolf Albert;

65 T: courtesy PAA (A2046); B: courtesy Vic Post Photography;

66 Steve Makris, courtesy *The Edmonton Journal*;

67 courtesy PAB;

68 courtesy PAB;

69 courtesy PAB;

70 courtesy PAB (Bl.891);

71 T: courtesy Rolf Albert; B: courtesy PAB;

72 TL: courtesy PAA (A3353); TR: courtesy GAI (NC-6-1311); UM: courtesy PAA (A3718); LM: courtesy PAA (A3462); BL: courtesy GAI (NC-6-3143); BR: courtesy PAA (A3355);

73 courtesy PAB;

74 courtesy Rolf Albert;

75 courtesy PAB;

76 courtesy PAB;

77 T: courtesy Rolf Albert; B: courtesy PAB;

78 courtesy PAB;

79 courtesy PAB;

80 courtesy Legislative Press Gallery;

81 courtesy PAB;

82 T: courtesy Legislative Press Gallery; B: courtesy PAB;

83 courtesy Legislative Press Gallery;

84 courtesy PAB;

85 courtesy PAB;

86 courtesy Rolf Albert;

87 courtesy PAB;

88 TL: courtesy PAB; BR: courtesy Vic Post Photography;

89 T, BR: courtesy PAB;

90 TL, TR, B: courtesy PAB;

91 T: courtesy Rolf Albert; B: courtesy PAB;

92 TL: courtesy GAI (NC-6-160); TC: courtesy PAB;

93 TR: courtesy PAA; B: courtesy PAB;

94 T: courtesy PAB; B: courtesy PAB;

95 T: courtesy PAB; B: courtesy PAB;

96 L: courtesy PAB; R: courtesy PAB;

97 courtesy PAB;

98 courtesy PAB;

99 TL, TR, M: courtesy PAB; B: courtesy Rolf Albert;

100 courtesy PAB.

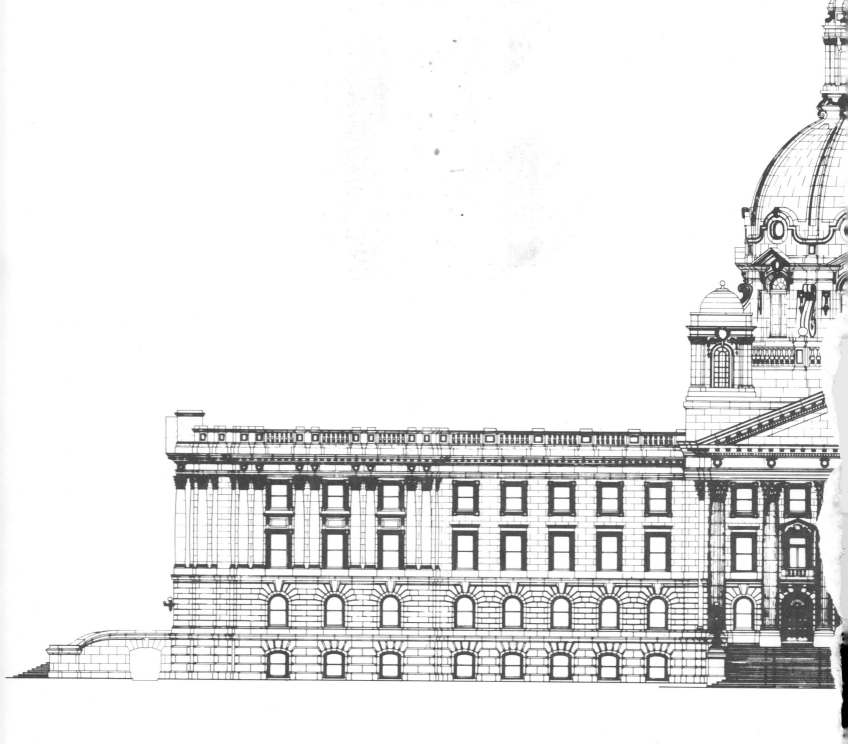